Promoting Learning for Bi[lingual]
Pupils 3–11

Promoting Learning for Bilingual Pupils 3–11

Opening Doors to Success

Edited by Jean Conteh

Paul Chapman
Publishing

Paul Chapman Publishing
A SAGE Publications Company
1 Oliver's Yard
55 City Road
London EC1Y 1SP

SAGE Publications Inc
2455 Teller Road
Thousand Oaks, California 91320

SAGE Publications India Pvt Ltd
B-42, Panchsheel Enclave
Post Box 4109
New Delhi 110 017

Library of Congress Control Number: 2006901363
A catalogue record for this book is available from the British Library

ISBN-10 1-4129-2083-3   ISBN-13 978-1-4129-2083-4
ISBN-10 1-4129-2084-1   ISBN-13 978-1-4129-2084-1 (pbk)

Typeset by C&M Digitals (P) Ltd., Chennai, India
Printed on paper from sustainable resources
Printed and bound in Great Britain by Cromwell Press, Trowbridge, Wiltshire

Contents

Foreword

Ros Garside, Achievement Manager, Education Bradford

This book provides excellent support for everyone who is involved in the education of bilingual learners. All teachers and other professionals will find that it contains practical approaches which they can adapt to their own classrooms and in planning at whole-school level. Jean Conteh and her fellow contributors have extensive experience of teaching children who are learning English as an additional language and of educating teachers in this field. They present a clear overview of the issues related to the teaching and learning of bilingual pupils, beginning with attitudes to and understandings of bilingualism. The book rightly emphasizes the importance of valuing the languages and cultures of all children and their families and demonstrates how these are an asset in learning English and in effective learning across the curriculum. Moreover, the principles and practices advocated in the book meet the needs of all pupils and not just bilingual learners.

The book provides practical advice for ensuring the best quality educational provision for bilingual children and their families. Classroom strategies are described in detail by teachers in their own words. The book includes approaches to the promotion of positive links between home and school. The strong focus on speaking and listening in the early years is carried into the chapter that introduces the link between talk and writing. This link is reinforced by chapters on bilingual approaches and the role of drama in promoting learning. Finally, issues of diversity and cohesion are considered in relation to schools with few bilingual learners.

Much of the experience on which this book is based comes from work in schools and colleges in Bradford, where a large minority of the population is bi-or multilingual. The educational achievement of these pupils and their future economic prosperity is central to the success and cohesion of Bradford District as a whole. Education Bradford is committed to multilingual approaches in the classroom and to supporting the central role of families in their children's education, and it supports the approaches advocated in this book. Education Bradford has also advocated a strong emphasis on speaking and listening, including the development of Talking Partners and bilingual approaches to drama. Bradford is a very diverse district and has schools with large minority ethnic populations, very mixed schools and schools with very few bilingual learners. Chapter 7, on promoting a positive ethos is highly relevant locally and includes a section on how schools across the district have formed links with contrasting schools. All schools need to recognize the language diversity and language variety of their particular pupils and to value the richness of their local areas, of Britain and of the wider world.

Acknowledgements

All the contributors to this book wish to acknowledge and thank the pupils, students, teachers and parents with whom they have shared teaching and learning over the years, and whose creative energies and enthusiasm underpin the ideas in this book. Jean wishes to thank her family for their patience and proofreading skills.

Note on royalties

All royalties earned by the sale of this book will be donated to the Bilingual Learning and Teaching Association, to which some of the contributors belong. Since 2003, the BLTA has been running Saturday classes for primary children and working with parents in Bradford to promote bilingual approaches to learning in order to help raise children's confidence as learners and their achievements in mainstream school. Further information about the BLTA can be found on: www.blta.org/.

Contributors

Shila Begum: Shila came to UK from Bangladesh with her family at the age of five. She gained a PGCE in 2001 with a specialism in the early years. She has worked since then as a teacher in Bradford in mainstream schools and also with the Bilingual Learning and Teaching Association, which seeks to promote the learning of bilingual pupils in schools.

Kathryn Bownass: Kathryn studied at Leeds Metropolitan University, qualifying with a BEd, General Primary in July 2000. She has taught at St Andrews' Primary, Keighley since 2001. In 2004 she participated in producing a *Speaking Listening and Learning* DVD for Education Bradford.

Avril Brock: After gaining a wealth of experience as an early years teacher and deputy head in schools in West Yorkshire, mainly in multilingual settings, Avril began work as a teacher-trainer and early years specialist at Bradford College in 1991. She now works as a Senior Lecturer in the School of Childhood and Community at Leeds Metropolitan University. She has published several articles and an edited book, *Into the Enchanted Forest* (Trentham Books, 1999).

Jean Conteh: After spending 14 years living and working in West Africa, Jean worked for 15 years in Bradford as a primary teacher and teacher-trainer. She now works in teacher education at the University of Manchester. Between 2000 and 2004 she developed a series of reading books for African primary schools – *Reading Worlds*, published by Macmillan. Other publishing includes a book for Trentham Books, *Succeeding in Diversity: Culture, Language and Learning in Primary Classrooms* (2003), which was nominated 'Book of the Week' by the *Times Educational Supplement*.

Ishrat Dad: Ishrat was born and went to school in Bradford. She gained a BEd Hons in 1997 with a specialism in Language and Literature. She has worked since then in a primary school on the outskirts of Bradford, where she is PE manager. She was seconded for two years to Bradford College to work with teacher-trainees to develop their understanding of language issues and of bilingualism. She also teaches English to 14–18 year-olds from various European countries.

Shirley Davids: Shirley has worked in a variety of Bradford schools for over 20 years. During this time she gained a MSc in Education Studies at Bradford University. She was asked to contribute to Education Bradford's *Speaking Listening and Learning* training materials whilst working with bilingual pupils in Keighley. She now works in Haworth Primary School.

Alex Fellowes: Alex worked in Africa as an English teacher, and has since worked for almost 30 years in Bradford as a teacher, deputy head of a middle school and as a teacher-trainer. He now spends most of his time developing drama projects with students and children of all ages, and has been invited to run courses with the RSC. He published a book for Trentham Books in 2001, *Bilingual Shakespeare*, which describes his work with middle school pupils over the years.

Angie Kotler: Angie started teaching in Tower Hamlets, spent eight years teaching and developing in-service training for primary teachers in Zimbabwe and moved to Bradford in 1991. She worked as a Reading Recovery Tutor and subsequently developed the Talking Partners scheme, which is now used nationwide. Angie co-authored a set of reading books for bilingual pupils in Bradford, called *Imran and Co*. She manages the Schools Linking Project, which is now in its fourth year.

Maggie Power: After teaching in Africa and London, Maggie moved to Bradford in the 1980s. She began working on drama projects with parents and children and moved to primary class teaching after a few years. She has worked for the past six years at Bradford College, teaching Language Education, RE and Drama. She has been involved in many projects using stories to encourage parental involvement and children's learning.

Chapter 1

Introduction: Principles and Practices for Teaching Bilingual Learners

Jean Conteh and Avril Brock

In this book we provide principles, advice and practical ideas for promoting the learning of bilingual pupils in mainstream primary schools, including children in the Foundation Stage. Most of the ideas and activities presented in the following chapters are from teachers and teacher-trainers who have worked for many years in schools in Bradford. In some Bradford schools, as in other cities in the UK, the majority of pupils are bilingual, and many are the children, grandchildren and even great-grandchildren of people who arrived to work in mills and factories 40 or 50 years ago. But there are also schools where bilingual pupils are very much in the minority, and where children have recently arrived from many different countries, including Eastern European and African countries. The guidance in this book is designed to cover both kinds of school setting.

We believe that the basic principles for promoting learning for bilingual pupils are the same, in many ways, as those for all pupils, so the first and over-arching principle for promoting learning is:

Good practice for bilingual learners is good practice for all learners

But, beyond these basic principles, there are important and distinctive features of bilingual learners' experiences that need specific support, and these are our main focus in this book.

In this chapter, we introduce the main ideas that flow through the book. We discuss:

- The centrality of language in learning
- Who are 'bilingual learners'? – definitions of bilingualism
- Language repertoires
- Links between first language and additional languages
- Transitional and additive bilingualism
- Whole-school benefits of bilingualism
- Key principles for planning teaching to promote additive bilingualism
- Translating principles into practice.

In Chapters 2–7, the principles are then developed and illustrated with a wealth of practical examples. Teachers who have carried out successful projects share their experiences and analyse what made their work successful. Words printed in **bold** in the text are explained in the Glossary, which begins on page 103. You will find full details of books and other resources mentioned in the chapters in the *further reading* sections at the end of each chapter.

THE CENTRALITY OF LANGUAGE IN LEARNING

Language is all around us, we hear and see language in the home, in the media, in the street, as well as in the school environment. Language forms the essence of thought; it is the medium in which understanding occurs. Through language, we construct our understanding of the world and are able to communicate with others. Language does not just occur in school as a body of knowledge in the subject called English or in the Literacy Hour. It is cross-curricular and forms the basis of learning in all the other curriculum areas. Language underpins learning, so, for young bilingual learners who are new to English, not only are they:

learning a new language

they are also

using language to learn new things.

This, of course, is true for all pupils, but it is more significant for pupils who enter school with very little English. It is essential that bilingual pupils have as much opportunity as possible to develop concepts in their first language, so that their learning is based on a firm foundation. At the same time, equal access to English should be offered to all bilingual pupils from the start of their time in formal education.

Because language and learning are linked in these ways, it can be a complex matter to identify correctly the needs of young bilingual learners who have little English and are at the early stages of schooling. It is well known that many learners new to English need a 'silent period' – when a child does not speak or respond to others – in order to build up their knowledge of English and their underlying proficiency before they begin to speak. Language needs can seem like learning needs, and sometimes specific learning needs can go undetected. In this book, we are not dealing directly with assessing bilingual learners' needs, but we recognize how issues of assessment influence teaching in many different ways. An excellent book that deals directly with this area is *Assessing the Needs of Bilingual Pupils* (Deryn Hall et al., 2001).

WHO ARE 'BILINGUAL LEARNERS'?
DEFINITIONS OF BILINGUALISM

In government documentation, the term most commonly used for pupils who speak other languages besides English is **EAL** (English as an additional language) learners. When we use the term 'bilingual' in this book, we are including EAL learners. We prefer the term 'bilingual' because we believe it is broader and more inclusive, and represents more accurately the important idea that, for bilingual children, all their languages contribute to their whole language experience and their knowledge of the world. Languages are not separate and isolated units. Bilingual children and adults naturally switch and mix between the languages they have at their disposal, they do not keep each language separate.

If you listen to groups of bilingual people having a conversation, you will often hear English words, phrases or sentences amongst the other languages they are using. This is known as **codeswitching**, and is especially common in children whose families have been settled in the UK for two or three generations, and who still maintain strong links with their homeland. Children from such bilingual (or multilingual) families will often speak different languages with different family members as a perfectly normal part of their lives; they may speak English with their siblings and perhaps their parents, but they will speak the family language (perhaps Urdu, Punjabi, Bangla, or Gujerati) with uncles, aunts and grandparents.

In talking about bilingualism in this way, we are not intending to suggest that children are fluent in all the languages they speak and write, but that – like the majority of people in the world – they have access to more than one language in normal and natural ways in their daily lives. The following, from Deryn Hall's book (2001), which she calls a 'working definition', is helpful in understanding the experiences of bilingual children in schools in England:

> In England the term is currently used to refer to pupils who live in two languages, who have access to, or need to use, two or more languages at home and at school. It does not mean that they have fluency in both languages or that they are competent and literate in both languages. (2001: 5)

This way of thinking about bilingualism, as 'living in two or more languages', makes clear the links between language and **identity**. An understanding of these links is very important for success in education. Our identities are formed from the activities we do every day and the conversations we have with the people around us. Through this, we develop a sense of where we belong, and of how we identify with the social worlds that surround us. There is a great deal of evidence to show that, if pupils feel they belong in the classroom and that their teachers value them as individuals, their attitudes to learning will be much more positive, and their achievement will improve.

Official statistics currently state the numbers of bilingual children in schools in England to be about 10%, or around 650,000 children, with almost 300 languages represented. These figures are partly based on the 2001 census where, for the first time, as a population we were asked to declare our ethnicities. But, there was no specific question on the census form about the languages we speak, so the official figures are based more on information about **ethnicity** than about language. It is likely that there will be questions specifically about language on the next census forms in 2011, which will be the first time that systematic information about the languages spoken and written by the people of Britain has been collected.

Even though the ethnic minority population of Britain is currently about 10% and so quite small, DfES statistics reveal that virtually all secondary schools and about 75% of primary schools have some learners who can be defined as bilingual on roll. Of course, the proportions vary considerably, with a few primary and secondary schools in cities like Bradford having virtually 100% bilingual pupils, and other schools having perhaps only a few bilingual learners.

Whatever the number and proportion of bilingual learners in your school or class, the principles for enhancing their learning remain the same. An essential starting-point is to make sure you have accurate information about the languages they speak, read and write. It is very important that every school with bilingual pupils finds out as much as possible about their pupils' home and community languages – this should be done as a matter of routine with all pupils as they begin school. There is a form in Chapter 7 (page 90) which you can use to do this.

LANGUAGE REPERTOIRES – WE ARE ALL 'BILINGUAL'

In official policy, pupils tend to be categorized as either 'monolingual' or 'bilingual'. It is important to remember, however, that many children who may not be categorized as bilingual have knowledge and experience of languages or of varieties of English that are different from those they will use and learn in school. Outside school, they may hear and use different **dialects** of English, which have grammar and vocabulary different from **standard English**. They and their families may speak in different **accents** from the ones most commonly used in school. In fact all of us, whether we regard ourselves as bilingual or monolingual, have language **repertoires**; we all have access to different ways of speaking and writing which we can choose from. We make our choices according to the following factors:

- Whom we are speaking to or writing for
- What we are trying to say or write
- Why we are trying to say or write these things
- When we are speaking or writing
- Where we are speaking or writing

So, for example, we speak in very different ways and about very different things to our families at home after a tiring day at work, to our colleagues in the staffroom at lunchtime, to pupils in the classroom or to friends whom we may meet on social occasions. We read different things in very different ways: planning files, novels, emails, bank statements, letters and so on.

This notion of language repertoires is a very useful one in helping to understand how language works and in thinking about how teaching can be made more focused and effective. If we help pupils to understand the '5Ws' (the who, what, why, when and where) of any language task they are expected to do, then their learning will be more meaningful, purposeful and – we hope – more successful.

Learning in different contexts

It is important to remember that, for many bilingual learners, formal learning does not end when they go home from their mainstream school in the afternoon. Many attend other schools in mosques, synagogues, churches, temples and other places in the community. They learn to read and write their family languages and the languages of their religions. Many students go on to take GCSE and A-level exams in Urdu, Gujerati, Bangla, Polish, Chinese and so on.

So, many bilingual pupils experience learning in different contexts. But often, their teachers in one context know very little about what goes on in the other, and it is the children who are making sense for themselves of very diverse learning experiences. As well as finding out about the languages that the pupils in your class speak, it is very worthwhile to find out about the different schools they attend, and what they are learning there. This will make them feel that you are interested in them and value them as individuals, and will also increase your knowledge of your pupils' home and community experiences. One Year 6 boy, who was interviewed as part of a research project, talked about his learning in a very insightful way, describing the different things his teachers did in his mosque school and his mainstream school. He ended with a very simple and heartfelt comment:

> 'I think the mosque and school should be together ... it's like the same thing ... you're teaching something, you're getting knowledge from people ...'

LINKS BETWEEN FIRST LANGUAGE AND ADDITIONAL LANGUAGES

First language acquisition begins at birth and continues through to at least the age of 12. Throughout our adult lives, we continue acquiring new vocabulary and grammatical structures. In turn, second language acquisition is a complex process, though some people would like to think it is fairly simple for young children. It takes place over a long time. In order for a second language to be truly additional rather than a replacement of the first, the first language needs to be maintained, encouraged and valued alongside the new language. Children need the space and opportunity to communicate with other people in their first language. They need to make connections and negotiate meanings to understand the world around them and to construct new knowledge. Many researchers emphasize the need for instruction to begin in the child's first language, so that a strong cognitive foundation can be developed, which forms the basis for academic learning. Competence in the first language is a good foundation for competence in additional languages.

Also, as we have already described, it is important for our self-confidence and identity as learners that we feel we belong and are valued in the settings in which we are learning. Bilingual children need to feel that their first language is valued in school and that it is not seen as second rate to English. Children will often be using the first language in the home situation, so it is a large part of their social lives, as well as being the main constituent of their thought processes in the early stages of learning English. If, as a teacher, you do not share your pupils' languages, you can do a lot to enhance their self-esteem and show that you value their languages through using dual language texts, multilingual labels in the environment and stories from their own and other cultures. Resources such as these also help children to transfer their thinking from one language to another.

TRANSITIONAL AND ADDITIVE BILINGUALISM

We use the word 'promoting' in the title of this book deliberately. We are hoping that the book will help all those involved in teaching bilingual learners to go beyond the model of 'language support' which was very common in the past and is implied in much official documentation. This model is based on the idea that we need to use home languages in school only to help bilingual learners gain confidence in English. But then, when their English reaches a suitable level, they do not need to use their other languages for learning any more and the bilingual support can be removed. We believe that this leads to **transitional bilingualism** in pupils, where their knowledge of English replaces rather than grows from their knowledge of other languages. Research has shown that transitional bilingualism can lead to restricted concept development and problems with learning.

Instead of this, we are advocating a model that promotes **additive bilingualism**. We hope that the ideas in this book will help teachers to value, enhance, encourage and develop their pupils' bilingualism, so that their knowledge of English becomes part of their ever-growing language repertoire, and not a replacement for proficiency in their other languages. We believe that this is the best way to really help bilingual pupils learn to their fullest capacity and achieve the best results they possibly can, as they progress through the school system. There is a great deal of research that supports this idea, such as the work of Jim Cummins (2001) and his associates, and many others. These are some of the key findings from research into bilingualism that have important implications for the classroom:

- Bilingual children often have greater cognitive capacity and awareness of language as a system than monolingual children.
- Many bilingual learners have increased self-confidence because they operate across different cultures and social groups.
- Children take up to two years to develop 'basic interpersonal communication skills' (**BICS**) but up to seven years to develop 'cognitive academic language proficiency' (**CALP**) (see page 10 for discussion of BICS and CALP).
- A 'silent period' at the early stages of learning an additional language is natural and normal, and not a sign that something is wrong.
- The first language is a valuable support for learning, and *not* something that interferes with the new language. Children will learn best through using and developing the full range of languages in their repertoires.
- It is not necessarily the case that the longer you spend learning a new language, the better the learning will be; time is clearly important, but not the only factor needed for successful language learning.
- Parents and families should be encouraged to share language and literacy with children in whatever languages they are most comfortable – learning new things first in the family languages will make the learning in an additional language easier and stronger.

In Chapters 2–7, you will find a wealth of suggestions for activities based on these ideas to help promote learning for bilingual pupils.

WHOLE-SCHOOL BENEFITS OF BILINGUALISM

There is little doubt that helping pupils to achieve additive bilingualism has many benefits for individual pupils themselves, but it also needs to be

Benefits for bilingual pupils:

1. Supports conceptual development at all stages
2. Enhances cognitive potential
3. Raises self-esteem and self-confidence as learners
4. Helps to form bridges between home and school experiences
5. Improves life chances and opportunities

Benefits for ALL pupils:

1. Increases language awareness and knowledge about language
2. Increases awareness of cultural diversity
3. Contributes to combating racism in school and wider community
4. Improves communication between different groups

Basic principles:

1. Promotes equality of opportunity for all pupils
2. Builds on the knowledge and experiences that pupils bring to school
3. Responds positively to diversity in society

Benefits for the whole school:

1. Increases knowledge about pupils and their communities
2. Recognizes pupils' families and communities as resources for learning in school
3. Increases awareness among teachers of language and cultural diversity
4. Strengthens links between school, home and community
5. Contributes to a stronger ethos for equality and diversity in school

Figure 1.1   The benefits of promoting bilingualism in school (adapted from the Schools Council's 'Mother Tongue Project', 1984)

recognized that it has considerable benefits for *all* pupils, for the school as a whole and the wider society. Figure 1.1, adapted from the Schools Council's 'Mother Tongue Project' from 1984, sums up the ways in which promoting additive bilingualism can benefit the whole school.

While it is clearly very important to plan activities in classrooms for individual pupils and groups of pupils, we need to do more than this to promote bilingualism in school. It needs to be seen as part of a wider concern to promote a whole-school ethos in which all pupils are valued, their individual strengths nurtured and their individual needs met. If this is the case, in a school in which bilingualism is promoted, *all* pupils will benefit, not just those who are themselves bilingual. This is discussed in Chapter 7.

KEY PRINCIPLES FOR PLANNING TEACHING TO PROMOTE ADDITIVE BILINGUALISM

In this book, we are focusing on classroom strategies and approaches for promoting additive bilingualism, and it needs to be remembered that, to be fully successful, these must be seen as part of positive whole-school and wider national policies. In 2003, Education Bradford published a Policy on Multilingualism, which provides a framework for promoting a positive whole-school ethos and developing whole-school policies to underpin bilingual approaches in classrooms. Here are the key principles they developed for promoting bilingualism in schools:

- English is the primary language of education and communication in this country. Therefore all children have a right to effective teaching of English and in English.
- Support in all the languages in a child's repertoire helps to ensure that children have the best access to new concepts and ideas and therefore to the highest possible achievement. It is essential that this starts with a strong foundation in the early years and continues as children grow older.
- Language is a fundamental aspect of identity. Acknowledging and promoting children's ability to communicate in their home languages builds self-confidence and encourages pupils' belief in themselves as learners.
- Access to a range of languages increases social and community cohesion and is an entitlement for all pupils. An ability to communicate in more than one language is a social and life advantage.
- Promoting home languages at school and within the school's community, including communicating with parents in ways that are accessible to them, builds community links and mutual respect. This encourages families and schools to work in partnership to develop children's full range of language competencies.
- Awareness of the systems and structures of one language aids the learning of other languages.
- Achievement in more than one language develops the capacity to enjoy being a confident and competent user of spoken and written language for an expanding range of purposes.
- The approach to language development is inclusive and values the language heritages and experiences of all pupils and adults within the educational community.

Based on these whole-school principles, we have developed a set of key principles for planning and carrying out activities, which we believe should underpin bilingual learning at all stages in primary schools. You will find that these principles are woven into all the practical ideas and strategies discussed in Chapters 2–7. Together, they provide a useful checklist of criteria for planning and implementing effective teaching activities for bilingual learners. Placed together here in a list, they can be photocopied and used as a checklist for your medium-term planning, to ensure that the work you plan offers as many opportunities as possible for promoting learning for your pupils:

Principles for planning activities for bilingual learners

1. Support in the first language and opportunities to use it for themselves in different ways in their everyday classroom activities will open out potential for learning for bilingual pupils.

2. Promoting home languages at school is an important way to support home–school links, and encourages families and schools to work in partnership.

3. Talk is one of the most important channels and tools for learning; pupils construct their knowledge in the classroom in all subjects through talk and so need every possible opportunity to explore ideas and concepts through talk, not just in English and the Literacy Hour.

4. The best writing develops from powerful and meaningful personal experiences, usually mediated by talk – before beginning extended writing activities, pupils always need the chance for collaborative discussion and planning.

5. Knowledge of more than one language promotes awareness of language systems and structures; this awareness needs to be supported and can be used as a valuable teaching and learning tool.

6. All learning, and especially language learning, is enhanced and strengthened by opportunities for hands-on experience.

TRANSLATING PRINCIPLES INTO PRACTICE

In this section, we show how these principles can be turned into practice, in two main ways:

- Contextualizing learning for bilingual pupils
- Providing a language-rich environment for learning.

Contextualizing learning

Principles 3, 4, 5 and 6, especially, point to the importance of *contextualizing learning* for bilingual pupils. It is vital to provide **contexts** for bilingual pupils' learning, and contexts are constructed through **scaffolding**. Learning is essentially an interaction between what the learner already knows and the new knowledge to be learnt, and contextualizing this process in familiar and stimulating settings makes it much more effective, as well as more interesting. Children's motivation, curiosity and willingness to learn are stimulated by the learning environment. Their attention is captured by what things look, smell, feel, sound and taste like and this needs to be taken into account in planning language activities. Avril Brock's book *Into the Enchanted Forest* (1999) illustrates this perfectly through describing a range of different activities in science as well as language learning that took place in a richly imaginative setting.

Young language learners need to be moved continually from the concrete to the abstract, supported at every level through first-hand experience. It is the talk that takes place around the activity which helps this to happen. Oral story is a very powerful vehicle for shaping language in very purposeful and interesting ways. Through the story, bilingual pupils can be introduced to new and complex language, contextualized in a meaningful and enjoyable experience.

Figure 1.2 illustrates the four stages in the move from concrete to abstract (or context-embedded to context-disembedded) thinking, and the kinds of activities and resources that support the transition across the stages.

Language is inherent in every curriculum area task. At times, especially in reading and writing tasks, all meaning will be expressed exclusively through oral and written forms of language. In context-embedded, face-to-face communication, meaning can be negotiated and is enhanced with a range of paralinguistic, situational and context cues. Bilingual pupils need these meaningful contexts to develop surface fluency (BICS), which is necessary to develop interpersonal communicative competence. At the same time these contexts provide a basis for the acquisition of academically related aspects of language necessary for higher-order cognitive proficiency (CALP), which is needed for children to develop and operate in the skills of literacy and the language for problem-solving.

Language used in educational settings is sometimes unique to that context and it may be difficult to transfer it to other situations or contexts. Context-reduced situations sometimes rely entirely on linguistic cues to convey meaning, with no additional contextual support. In settings such as these, it helps if children can work, talk and listen in small groups, as this makes it easier for each person to understand, concentrate and make contributions. Cummins suggests that providing bilingual pupils with tasks that are both cognitively demanding and yet firmly embedded in context, ensures a more successful

Concrete primary experiences	Contextualized secondary experiences	Two-dimensional experiences	Abstract situations
Multi-sensory	Multi-sensory	Single sense (usually seeing or hearing)	Symbols
Visits Experimentation	Drama Role play Models, Toys Videos	Pictures Flash cards Cut outs Diagrams Maps	Discussion Writing messages

Figure 1.2 **Moving children from the concrete to the abstract in their thinking and learning**

communication of ideas, since learners will be able to rely on a wide range of situational cues in order to negotiate meaning.

Beginning with context-embedded activities and gradually moving, with talk and action, towards less embedded activities means that children are never left without support, and at the same time are being encouraged to move to the new knowledge which is the object of the activity. This additional contextual and linguistic support is what we mean by scaffolding. Scaffolding can be developed through a variety of practical resources and multi-sensory experiences, including – again – story. Scaffolding is developed through talk. Pauline Gibbons' work (2002) shows how teachers can provide scaffolds for their pupils through their talk, and her ideas are fully illustrated with practical examples in Chapter 4.

Providing a language-rich environment

Principles 1, 2, 4 and 5 point to the need for a language-rich learning environment. Teachers of bilingual pupils are often concerned that their pupils will struggle to understand language which they feel may be too difficult, such as complicated sentences and vocabulary in English. They feel that their pupils have 'limited vocabulary' or a very narrow range of language experience. This concern is sometimes fed more by teaching materials and curriculum guidance than by the pupils themselves. The opposite is more likely to be true. A great deal of research shows that 'bilinguals' potentially have much greater awareness and understanding of language than 'monolinguals' (this is sometimes called **metalinguistic awareness**). This language awareness can be used as a powerful resource for learning, for both bilingual and monolingual children. Children can be encouraged to compare words and their meanings in different languages, and to think about how the grammars of languages can differ. There are some suggestions for this kind of work in Chapter 5.

In order to promote language awareness, it is important to provide a rich and stimulating language environment for bilingual pupils – indeed, for all pupils. One of the ways of doing this is to develop a 'rich scripting' approach to planning and carrying out activities, in all subjects across the curriculum. Such an approach is explained and illustrated in Norah McWilliam's book, *What's in a Word?* (1998), and ideas taken from this book are woven into the activities described in most of the chapters that follow, especially Chapters 3 and 4.

CONCLUSION

To sum up, children need to be:

- Motivated to want to learn
- Supported in their learning through first-hand experiences
- Moved continually from the concrete situation to the abstract situation through talk
- Involved in context-embedded experiences such as story, which promote the target language in rich and meaningful ways
- Prompted to talk about what they are doing at every stage of the activity
- Given models of the target language, and the ways it is used in context
- Given opportunity to formulate their own questions and answers related to the activity
- Encouraged to develop awareness by talking explicitly about word meaning, grammar and other features of different languages.

FURTHER READING

Brock, Avril (ed.) (1999) *Into the Enchanted Forest – Language, Drama and Science in Primary Schools.* Stoke-on-Trent: Trentham Books.

Cummins, Jim (2001) *Negotiating Identities: Education for Empowerment in a Diverse Society.* 2nd edn. Ontario, CA: California Association for Bilingual Education.

Gibbons, Pauline (2002) *Scaffolding Language, Scaffolding Learning: Teaching Second Language Learners in the Mainstream Classroom.* London: Heinemann.

Hall, Deryn, Griffiths, Dominic, Haslam, Liz and Wilkin, Yvonne (2001): *Assessing the Needs of Bilingual Pupils: Living in Two Languages.* 2nd edn. London: David Fulton.

McWilliam, Norah (1998) *What's in a Word?* Stoke-on-Trent: Trentham Books.

Chapter 2

Promoting Positive Links Between Home and School

Maggie Power and Avril Brock

This chapter discusses the importance of positive home–school links throughout primary school for promoting bilingual children's learning, and explains how schools can develop such links through recognizing and valuing the diversity of ways in which parents support their children at home.

Specific examples are given of strategies and activities that have been shown to help promote effective, two-way home–school links. We use the words and ideas of teachers who have successfully employed different approaches to develop positive links with parents to show how the ideas can be turned into practice in school.

RESPECTING AND LISTENING

We begin with an acrostic of a very important word. The letters spell out a message that is a guide for working not only with bilingual children, but with all children:

RESPECT

Reach out to expand and extend knowledge of the community, the family, and the child
Expect achievement equal to all
Show openness and a willingness to listen
Provide open doors through which resources and support can be acquired
Encourage, go towards others – do not expect them to have the confidence to enter
Contact and affirm: ring, write, email and offer praise to encourage
Together set targets so together success can be celebrated

Education should be about service, about giving, and knowing, respecting and enriching the children in our care. As a teacher, you need to have your eyes and ears open to the children that come through the door of the school and then the classroom. Those children need time to talk, time to be themselves and to bring something of what there is within their lives into the room, and what they bring, what they share, needs to be listened to, not just by the teacher but by the other children as well.

All of us need to be aware that we are there to encourage, develop and empower the children, to equip them in such a way that they can function and grow throughout their lives. We must start in all of our schools by creating space, space to listen, because when we do not create space to listen the results can be tragic. One teacher recounted an incident that showed how one child had had no space to speak and to share.

> 'A child arrived in school, and was dropped into the busyness of a Monday morning – into the "this is your target, these are our objectives, these are the words you need to learn by break time". He did what he could and it was only at break time that, holding the hand of a colleague on duty, he was able to share the sad experiences of the weekend. His family had been involved in an accident in which his grandfather had suddenly died. The tragedy for the child and the family was immense but how sad, how failing of us in our institution and methodology that there was not even a moment at the start of a Monday morning for someone to have asked and listened, listened to what had happened to this little boy over the weekend.'

How can anyone working with young children work effectively without contact with the parents and key carers of the children?

OPENING DOORS – WAYS OF LEARNING

Schools must have established channels for communication with whoever brings the child into the school. There need to be open doors through which all can walk and the doors need to swing both ways.

All teachers need to be aware at all times of who the first teachers of the children are – parents and families. Most parents provide valuable interaction and meaningful experiences for their children. Children learn to walk and talk before they ever come near our schools, and we need to remember, of course, that they are introduced to much more. Families provide enrichment and nurturing and not just that which meets the physical needs of the children. Through the family, children learn what is right and wrong, what is acceptable behaviour. If you ask many Muslim children what they know about behaviour and about how they should relate to each other, they will talk about the angels that sit, one on each shoulder, writing and keeping a record of their deeds for the day of judgement. In talking and listening to children and recognizing our own need to learn, we can find out so much about what motivates the children in our care.

The open door is so important. The place and space for parents to come into school needs to be established for every day, not just for special events. Parents have the right and must feel that they have the opportunity to talk face to face with a sympathetic member of staff when they need to. Schools can also provide support and practical help. There can be:

- A toy library
- Access to books in a range of languages
- Literature in relation to health, legal services and other community provision
- Story sacks
- A noticeboard
- Provision for links to be made between parents or carers using ICT, email or webCT.

All of the above needs to be available in the languages of the home as well as the main language of the school.

For some mothers, the time in school is the one accepted time when they can be outside the home and are able to engage in learning for themselves. Many schools now have classes for parents and it is possible for them to be the springboard into additional learning and access to so much more. What is important is not just the provision of such classes but the continued ongoing support that makes it possible for mothers to drop in and out of them. There will always be the morning when someone is ill, when a child needs to be taken to an appointment. Parents must be valued for what they can do and not criticized for what they find difficult to fulfil.

PARENTAL EMPOWERMENT

Too often, we feel it is the experts in education who know what needs to be done. But we must recognize the importance of working in consultation to involve the parents in identifying what they need, and what they want to take from the sessions if their needs are to be met. Classes that focus on reading and on the parents learning to read and write in English are available in many schools. One teacher recalled how consulting the class members had interesting results:

'In our school the focus was on the mothers learning English. It deviated into how we all celebrate when it is a special time for us within our families. What developed was a valuable sharing of experiences and a sharing in the class of a number of meals, a Christmas dinner (using a halal chicken), an Eid celebration and so much more. What happened was that alongside the formal work the sharing enabled all to build up knowledge of the conventions and patterns of behaviour that governed celebration in each of the cultural groups.'

Another teacher developed what she did in the classes in response to ideas from the parents:

'The parents thought that rather than just reading together it would be helpful to them to use the books the children were learning to read from. The motivation for the parents was there, to be familiar with, to be comfortable with the book their child was asked to bring home and read from. This gave confidence, gave dignity to them in the home and helped their children. To know that you can hear a child read, can be a listener and someone capable of affirming your own child even if it is difficult for you to understand all of the text yourself – is just so important.'

Script and print need to be made available from a range of languages and genres that both affirm the children and increase the knowledge of those working in the school about the background of the children. Parents and carers can be involved in the selection of this written material, which then needs to be made available throughout the school, in the classrooms, in the school library and also in the staffroom.

The key principle underlying these educational endeavours is:

the need for the parent to feel valued.

Schools need to help parents feel that they have a place, a part to play in the education of their own child. It also needs to be understood that parents of any background can contribute to the decisions made in relation to a range of issues in any school. Parents can be involved in and contribute to assemblies, festivals, educational trips, parties and so much more. Parents need to have high expectations of their children and their teachers and an understanding that they have a part to play in working with and alongside the teachers in developing their children's learning.

In addition, schools can set up parent councils where, for instance, each class could be asked to select two parents who will meet at set times with the head-teacher and/or others to discuss not just issues and concerns, but what the school is doing well. This is a more formal way of involving members of the parent body. Put alongside parent representation on the governing body, it is a valuable way to support parents and staff as they work together.

ESSENTIAL CONTEXTS

Language and culture are central to family and identity. All teachers need to respond to individual children's needs, demonstrating an awareness, acceptance and consideration of children's cultural experiences and linguistic skills. As we explained in Chapter 1, over the past 30 years there has been a great deal of research demonstrating how the development of the first language accelerates the learning of a second. Ever since the Bullock Report of 1975, which asserted the importance of first language, schools have been expected increasingly to recognize that bilingualism is an asset, an extra advantage for children's learning.

Culture provides connecting links for children and offers a scaffolding of understanding. Children, like adults, learn through the mediation of others. Cultural experiences are powerful; through them, we interpret the world and its social conventions. Parents and grandparents are significant mediators for children in structuring their cultural knowledge and heritage and relating these to the world around them. Different cultures make meaning in different ways – the experiences children bring to the classroom are formed in social learning from the adults they live with. As teachers, we should encourage children to take on the role of experts providing cultural information and demonstrating their capability to work in more than one language when appropriate. In this way, we learn about their language, knowledge background and expertise and provide important stepping-stones to their further development and learning.

COMMUNITY STORIES – THE ORAL TRADITION

Stories form a part of many children's early experiences. But stories do not only exist in books. Teachers need to seek out the kinds of stories that exist outside of our normal story repertoires, in places where we may not expect to find them. Stories exist within communities, where they always have specific purposes. To discover the different stories children bring from home is to introduce another dimension into one's understanding of community, faith and value.

We all have stories that reflect our cultures. Children and parents can be asked to contribute stories under a number of headings. These stories often offer us implicit insight into guidance on how to behave, or how not to behave. Some will be tales concentrating on universal themes, such as what happens to liars. In Europe the main character might be looking after sheep, whereas from the Indian subcontinent it might be goats that need to be tended. The 'attackers' will be a tiger in one country and a wolf in another. The key point is to realize that stories, although they take many forms, can be shared in any language. The key skill of the teacher is to be open to them. It is to recognize the commonality of human experience and to be open to the considerable wisdom that there is within families whatever their backgrounds.

There are many different ways in which community stories can be collected and made part of the learning experiences in our classrooms. Here are a few examples for activities, with comments from teachers who have successfully carried them out.

Favourite family stories

Simply ask children to bring in a favourite family story from home. You can suggest a theme, or leave it open so that the children and their families can decide what is interesting to send. These could be from their national or personal story heritage.

In one school, this work led to a collection of stories sent in by families. Whole families, often across three generations, contributed to this collection. The work grew into a cornucopia, an opportunity to share positively heart-warming experiences as so many people in the community became involved. It resulted in the creation of a highly successful professional video entitled *Grannies*. This was a compilation of the children's grandmothers recounting their own stories and the children themselves telling stories. Some stories were personal and others were from their heritage; some storytellers dramatized their stories as plays and others performed shadow puppet shows of traditional folk tales. The stories were presented in both Punjabi and English. In the following extract the teacher involved in gathering the stories recounted one experience that occurred in her classroom:

'We had asked the children to ask their families for a favourite story. One child asked her grandmother for a story. The woman had not had access to formal education either in this country or in Pakistan where she had lived for much of her life but she was an excellent storyteller.

(Continued)

(Continued)

She told her granddaughter the story of two silly bulls who went in search of fresh grass to eat. In walking far away from their home they became vulnerable. They enjoyed the grass but then found themselves confronted by a large lion who then saw them as his tea. But brave and determined they faced him together and eventually forced him to retreat. They were able to return safe and secure to their home area – but sadly then began to argue about who was the bravest. As they each wanted to claim that they had been the saviour of the other, they decided that they would settle their argument by returning to meet the lion again. This they did and then to prove their worth they went forward one at a time to face and fight the lion. Without the strength of the other each was vulnerable, and the lion, who by this time is very hungry, was of course able to eat both.

The message for the granddaughter, her class and her class teacher was – alone you can achieve little but working together you are both stronger and better able to succeed in whatever you undertake. The process of gathering stories in this case reinforced an important message for all in our school.'

Stories of the past brought into the present

It is important to remember that some families will have arrived from areas of the world where there is conflict and forced movement of people. They also have stories to bring into the classroom. If people are able to share their stories in this way, this will reinforce for your pupils that stories take many different forms and that we can all respect the storytellers and gain from listening. Pupils can be involved in collecting information, listening to first hand accounts of events and then processing information so that they can share with others in a range of different ways, both oral and written. Stories and memoirs can be a source of stimulus for other work, for considering distance, for looking at an atlas to gain information about far away places, for writing poems – all of this is linked with real, lived experience which means that the quality of the learning is rich and firmly grounded.

Children themselves, no matter how young, come into our schools with a past history. This past covers their immediate experience and then goes back to all that has happened to them in their young lives. They also carry with them the past history and heritage of their families. This can be challenging but also enriching. Children in many of our schools have come from places and countries far away. They have stories to tell. Our classrooms need those narratives if we are to truly know and understand our communities.

In one Bradford inner city primary school the exploration of this community narrative linked language, history and geography learning in a curriculum project. The teacher leading the project recalled:

'As a staff we encouraged pupils to collect the personal stories of people linked to the school community. We gave the work the title – **Bradford is Our City**. Our objective was to find out how people in the school community came to be in the city. This involved initially asking the teachers and the other adults working in the school to share memories of how and when we or they had come to live in or be associated with the city. This

(Continued)

exercise became very quickly one of discovery, of gaining and sharing new knowledge about each other. It included a lunchtime supervisor who told of fleeing conflict in India at the time of partition; a teacher who shared the experience of political exile as part of the Hungarian community; another teacher told of economic migration from Eire when a very young child, but not so young as not to be affected by the experience of sounding different and being laughed at in a London school; a school social worker who had attended the same school when girls and boys went in through different entrances and were taught separately.

The experience the children gained in searching out this information from staff and other adults helped them to build bridges to their own lives. Many of the children's parents had travelled to Bradford from other places. Pupils were encouraged to talk to their parents about how they had come to Bradford.

This process involved in the work of exploring how people came to be in Bradford helped deepen a sense of community between the adults and the children. It developed an understanding, within both the pupil and adult communities, of the similarity in people's experiences. This is important if a sense of being part of the same community and identifying that we are a community, young and old with the same aspirations for the children in our care, is to be achieved.'

● Family trees

Children can be very good at understanding where they fit in relation to their wider family network. Ask them to provide a family tree. In one family tree project, a child who had uncles and aunts nearby and a number of cousins in the school, in order to construct her family tree, needed not just one more piece of paper, but another table on which to put the many other pieces of paper she had filled!

Children often have an extensive knowledge of their family and a sense of their identity in relation to their place within a network that can bridge a town or city and also reach out across country boundaries. There is more about family trees as a way of promoting a 'bilingual approach' to learning in Chapter 5 (page 69). Also, in Jean Conteh's *Succeeding in Diversity* (2003), there is an account of a fascinating 'name tree' activity, developed in a nursery by Suzanne Aston, a PGCE student. The activity, shown in the box, allows young children to explore their own names and family identities while meeting the language and literacy goals of the Foundation Stage.

Activity: Name tree

Suzanne began by showing the children a photo of her own daughter and explaining how she had chosen her name. She then gave a letter asking for some information about the child's name to each child to take home to their parents. These were available in Urdu as well as English. All parents responded positively. Some sent written notes into school and some spoke directly to Suzanne or the bilingual assistant. As the information came in, each child had a turn to talk about their name to the whole class. They were then helped to write the information onto a paper leaf for the name tree that had been put up ready on the wall. When appropriate, names were written in their original language and script. The child then hung their own leaf on the name tree. This took two weeks to complete. While it was going on, Suzanne introduced discussions about the names for different family members, illustrated her own family tree on the whiteboard and encouraged the children to talk about their families and to draw a family member.

By the end of the project, every child had confidently stood up in front of their peers and teachers to speak at length, listed attentively to their class-mates and taken part in discussions about family. The class also had an impressive name tree on display which parents were invited to see. Suzanne followed up the vocabulary development in more structured Literacy Hour-type activities, encouraging the children to read many of the words by sight.

Source: Jean Conteh, *Succeeding in Diversity*: *Culture, Language and Learning in Primary Classrooms* (Stoke-on-Trent: Trentham Books, 2003) reproduced with permission.

Simple written texts to widen knowledge

Another example of valuable work is linked to widening our knowledge of the world. As we travel, be it within the district or other parts of the country or the world, postcards can be sent back into the school, bringing the world into the classroom. Postcards can arrive in any language and script and be of value – if the language is a new one to the class, pupils can do some detective work to find out what it is and where it comes from. Children themselves, as they travel across the world to link up with family members, can be asked to send a card that they know will be read and cherished by friends at school. Their classmates can look at maps to find out where the card has travelled from, and compare it with where they are in the world.

Of course, books are important in any school classroom. The range and availability of published material in different languages is now such that it is possible to have books in many different scripts in all classrooms. Material can come from a number of different cultures and reflect the rich diversity of the country, the continent and so the world the children belong to. It is also important to acknowledge the importance of children seeing themselves represented in books. Books can be made with the children themselves as characters in them. For example, books about local places of worship or about shops and parks in the area, about local stories and events can be easily made. Parents can be supported in providing material and information to contribute to these books.

MAKING LINKS: TWO CASE STUDIES

There is also an important role to be played by outreach workers, community workers or home–school liaison workers who cross boundaries between home and school. The training they get to prepare them for such an important task needs always to stress the importance of positive affirmation. By the relationships they build between the child, the family and the school they have a vital task in strengthening the bonds between the three.

The following two case studies illustrate ways in which links can be made through workers in the community. The first, the 'Earlystart Project', describes highly effective and exciting work promoted in Bradford that involved outreach workers who provided access into education for young children and their families. The second, organized by a local college, focused on working with parents in school.

Case Study 1: Earlystart

Bradford's 'Earlystart' Project was a five-year Single Regeneration Budget (SRB), Government-funded initiative aimed at helping young children from families where English was not their first language, with speaking and understanding before they started school.

The aims of Earlystart were to:

- activate principles supported by the Bradford Early Years and Childcare Partnership and Bradford Integrated Services Plan;
- operate within a framework of equal rights and partnership with families and communities;
- respect families and communities, recognizing that the parent/carer is the first and constant teacher of the child;
- consult with the young children's families and communities it seeks to support;
- celebrate and value children's home languages, which are respected as part of their identity, supporting bilingualism as a positive asset, which should be embedded in a multilingual learning environment;
- recognize that children learn English best through concrete experience backed by extensive interaction with adults, particularly through play experiences.

The objectives of Earlystart were to promote the learning and achievement of young bilingual children aged 0–5 years through:

- outreach work from the four nursery schools involved, introducing home-based learning through play and books for babies in liaison with health visitors;
- early support and information to parents to enable them to take full advantage of nursery provision and be actively involved in their child's learning;
- early nursery groups for parents and to bridge the gap between home and nursery education;
- community and nursery-based parent education focusing on parenting, childcare and play, early literacy and numeracy;
- empowerment of parents.

The project aimed to raise achievement, not by bringing children into early years settings prematurely but by promoting developmentally appropriate experiences for them that were suitable and accessible for parents.

The outreach workers needed a range of skills, including:

▶

- knowledge of young children's development and need for play;
- ability to work with adults;
- sensitivity to cultural issues involved;
- particular bilingual skills – five languages were spoken by the outreach workers: Bangla, English, Gurmurki Punjabi, Punjabi, Urdu.

The role of the outreach worker was quite complex and involved visits into homes in the community, making links with parents, playing with the children as nursery nurses in the setting, teaching parenting classes, organizing resources. The outreach workers were very enthusiastic and committed.

The impact on parents and children

Parents stated how they were made to feel very welcome in school and had very positive attitudes about Earlystart. It boosted parental self-esteem and empowered parents, as they were able to understand more about the schooling process and found that they had a support system if they needed it. As one parent stated:

> 'We all think it is an important project ... all my family now want to get involved in his learning and think it is very important.'

Promoting learning through play

Parents developed an increasing awareness of the importance of learning through play and began to understand the value of helping their children learn through play. They told of how they had become more observant and interested in what their children were doing and what they were learning. Parents had really noticed the difference in their children's language, social and educational development and were confident about the achievements gained:

> 'I think it has made a big difference not only educationally, but also in the social aspect. I can see the difference between my child's stage of development and other children who have not been through the project.'

Promoting language and literacy

The children were more confident in English and in first language as a result of Earlystart:

> 'He is picking up a lot of English in comparison to other children who don't take part in the Earlystart project. In general his language skills have improved greatly. I also like it because they encourage my child to speak in our own language as well as English. I feel that this nursery values home language by helping to support bilingualism.'

Parents valued the use of dual language textbooks and felt bilingualism was being encouraged:

> 'I particularly like borrowing dual language books because my husband can't speak English but can read to our child in Bengali, which makes him feel involved.'

Further education and training for parents

Earlystart began to have an effect on parents moving towards gaining further education and training. Parents were undertaking professional development through participating in voluntary work, taking part in courses in the settings, home visits, enrolling on further education courses:

> 'The project has given me a lot of confidence and the motivation to take part in the courses. I also go with the outreach worker to home visits.'

Many adult classes now run in schools as a result of Earlystart. The headteachers were keen to offer training for parents:

> 'This is a valuable, beneficial addition to the project, which would further enhance home–school relationships and we intend to create accommodation for training at our nursery school.'

Transition into nursery

The targeting of pre-nursery-age children ensured that benefits were established and could be built on before the children started school. There was much better settlement into nursery and easier separation from parents. Children settled in more effectively because:

- they were already familiar with resources, books and toys and the building;
- they had the confidence to separate from their mother more readily;
- their play skills were better developed;
- their parents were more inclined to feel a sense of belonging to the nursery their child was entering;
- the children became familiar with other staff.

Nursery staff observed that Earlystart had promoted greater inter–school relations through encouraging beneficial relationships. As a headteacher commented:

> 'There are many positive effects. It has made staff more aware of the needs of under-3s. Long term, we have seen them develop from babies, we get to know the parents really well and also the whole family.'

In conclusion

As the project proved so successful with so many families, news of it spread rapidly by word of mouth and through the extended family network. Surestart followed on from the Earlystart procedures and the Local Authority disseminates the good practice it established. Surestart has now become firmly established in the SRB area and there was much interaction and involvement between the two projects. The empowerment of parents and the differences the Earlystart project made to families in feeling that they had an important role to play was clear.

The parents' involvement and their keen interest in their child's learning was overwhelming and it was inspiring as to what 'a little bit can do'. Earlystart was not a large project, but had obvious long–term beneficial effects for the families involved. As the nursery schools move towards becoming Children's Centres, the good practice established through Earlystart is set to continue.

Case Study 2 From school to college

Staff (including both authors) from a teacher training department, which is part of a large further and higher education college, worked with mothers over a number of years in an inner city school in the Manningham district of Bradford. The sessions provided each year varied, but the links established with the college meant that high quality teaching could be offered to the mothers. The themes explored over time all focused on the school curriculum and included:

- what is reading?
- the differences between decoding and reading for meaning and under-standing;
- identifying print in all languages represented in various ways in the community;
- approaches to valuing bilingualism;
- developing the young writer, the young scientist, the young mathematician at home.

The mothers were taken to the college to see where their children might go and study in the future if they wanted to enter further or higher educa-tion. Opportunities to meet and discuss with existing students were arranged as part of the programme.

Working with mothers: constructing learning and relationships

At the start of the project, there was no fixed set of aims, objectives, strate-gies or targets. We had the overall goal of developing a dialogue between home and school about children's learning, and, through this, empowering mothers to support their children's learning. We had two hours every Wednesday morning, and we negotiated the work we would do as we went along – all things were possible.

The mothers understood that if they were able to come that was celebrated, but that if family commitments got in the way, then this was recognized.

The school provided:

- someone to translate, often the home–school liaison officer but at other times one of the mothers was able to and was encouraged to translate for others;
- a friendly welcome that included a warm drink and biscuits and also juice for the pre-school children who accompanied their mothers;
- a child-friendly space with toys, books in a range of languages and scripts where children could play while we talked and worked.

In addition, the college provided materials: a folder containing a programme of what we would be doing over the four or six weeks that the group would meet and two books, *Send for Sohail!* and *The Balloon Detectives*, which had been produced by Bradford College. Both are exciting, dual language text books that gave the families something to share from the very first week. (There is an extract from *Send for Sohail!* in Chapter 3 of this book, see Figure 3.1, page 38.)

The sessions were planned to be both interactive and affirmative. The ideas and knowledge came from the mothers themselves. The following is a brief selection of some of the things that happened.

1. The mothers were very interested in languages, and we began with a discussion of what it meant to be bilingual, how that was the norm and not something unusual or a problem – indeed, most of the world is bilingual. We also considered the differences in attitude towards children who were bilingual French–English speakers as opposed to those who were Punjabi–English speakers. At times, teachers will regard the first as much more positive than the second, as this is the way they are led to regard them in curriculum and policy documents.
2. We looked at the value and importance of story/telling and sharing both at home and in school. Within this, there was time to tell and to dramatize and we had a classroom improvisation around a traditional tale, *Three Billy Goats*, which was universally popular. With a kind of shadow sharing activity, the teacher providing the words that were then echoed by the mother, we had some very excited goats and some fierce trolls!
3. We looked at print, at where it existed around us and where we could point it out to the children, find the patterns and share the excitement of discovery, in our streets, shops and kitchen cupboards. We talked about how we could be text detectives, and how this could support children's learning.
4. We looked at the importance of reading and the need to build confidence in our children and to nurture their interest. We talked about the different ways in which you can hear a child read and enjoy what they are doing, even if you have not had the opportunity to learn to read in that language yourself.

Each session ended with a task, something to consider and for the mothers to do with their family before the next session. Alongside this, the school staff both affirmed the parents and valued the work whenever possible, for example in talking with them about reading with their children, and encouraging them to try out ideas discussed in the sessions.

And as a final session, the mothers were introduced to the college. Transport was provided and they were taken on a visit where they were introduced to some young bilingual students who showed them around and shared their aspirations to study and gain professional jobs.

What was established throughout the project was the firm principle that both parents and teachers have a part to play with the school in educating their children. The teachers came to appreciate that there was a value for all in working in partnership. Possibly, some of the teachers' stereotypes were broken down as they discovered that, just as in middle class, more affluent areas where parents took an active role in supporting the work of the school, so could the parents of the children they taught. There was so much they could do and enjoy doing, once they were confident of their importance and the value of their part in what has to be seen as a three-way triangular relationship:

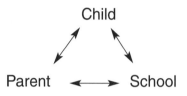

CONCLUDING THOUGHTS

Writing in his book *Schools of Hope*, Terry Wrigley quotes a declaration from a conference in Germany in 1995. The values it embodies underpin the ideas we have been discussing in this chapter, and provide a powerful vision of a school that genuinely promotes positive links between home and school.

The declaration states that a school is a house of learning:

- A place where everybody is welcome, where learners and teachers are accepted for their individuality
- A place where people are allowed time to grow up, to take care of one another and be treated with respect
- A place whose rooms invite you to stay, offer you the chance to learn and stimulate you to learn and show initiative
- A place where diversions and mistakes are allowed, but where evaluation in the form of feedback gives you a sense of direction
- A place for intensive work, and where it feels good to learn
- A place where learning is infectious.
  (Wrigley, 2003, p. 5)

As Wrigley says at the end of his book, we have not simply to improve schools but to rethink education, and surely we cannot do that successfully unless we involve the parents and the children in the task (2003, p. 183).

The summary box presents the main points of this chapter, and can be used as a basis for discussion in school in working out ways to improve home–school links.

Summary: Linking home and school developing partnerships

Schools need to:

- Respect and listen to parents
- Value different ways of learning
- Recognize the skills parents have
- Use the 'funds of knowledge' in the community to enhance their work in school
- Find opportunities to draw parents into school

Parents need to:

- Support the work of the school
- Recognize their own power and influence over their child
- Take opportunities offered by the school to get involved in their child's learning
- Keep the school informed of any problems or concerns with their child

---

FURTHER READING

Bastiani, John and Wolfendale, Sheila (eds) (1996) *Home–School Work in Britain: Review, Reflection and Development.* London: David Fulton.

Conteh, Jean (2003) *Succeeding in Diversity: Culture, Language and Learning in Primary Classrooms.* Stoke-on-Trent: Trentham Books.

Chapter 3

Promoting Learning in the Early Years

Avril Brock and Maggie Power

Through practical examples and suggestions, this chapter provides advice for teachers on helping young bilingual children make the transition from home to school and begin their formal or statutory education with confidence and enthusiasm. It stresses the importance of:

- Developing their self-confidence as learners
- Supporting their experiences with those at home
- Promoting their interest and enthusiasms for the routines and activities in which they will participate in nurseries and reception classes.

Specific ideas from contemporary practice in early years settings provide ideas for stimulating activities, purposeful experiences and ways of communicating with parents that will promote young bilingual children's learning.

In early years settings, professionals are adept at working in teams, which can include teachers, nursery nurses, assistants and others. In this chapter, when we talk about 'teachers', we are including all these educators of young children.

SUPPORTING THE YOUNG BILINGUAL CHILD

One of the key ideas underpinning this book is that culture, identity, knowledge, experience and language are all closely interwoven. Young bilingual children need to feel that their own language, culture and family experience are recognized and valued, with their religious beliefs, lifestyles and histories respected. Self-esteem, positive attitudes, social and emotional well-being are key aspects that need to be promoted for successful learning to occur. That family and community members are vital to the educational success of young bilingual children was firmly demonstrated in Chapter 2. The 'Earlystart Project' demonstrated how undertaking home visits can establish highly positive links between home and educational settings. In this way, not only is children's transition into more formal learning situations supported, so is the development of first and additional language learning and the promotion of a greater understanding of learning through play. Once parents have become involved in the early years of their children's education, they feel more encouraged to be involved in their children's education through the ensuing years. They have met teachers on the family terms in their homes and so gained a valuable point of contact. The home visits made such a difference in one inner city school that they now get 90% attendance at parents' evenings.

Young bilingual children need to feel that their first language is valued because it is a main constituent of their thought processes. In the home, with family, siblings and friends, they often use it for communication to negotiate meanings and so to understand the world around them. In making the transitions into the early years educational setting and into English, it is important to maintain the developing bilingual child's self-esteem. Young bilingual children need an environment where they can practise, explore, think and talk aloud. They need opportunities to talk in and beyond practical activities. They need to be able to make mistakes and feel that their attempts and opinions are taken seriously. Therefore children in the early stages of additional language acquisition require thoughtful consideration about their particular educational needs. The developing bilingual child may wish to stay silent until she or he feels competent to articulate in an additional language. Young bilingual children may:

- Not understand every word of what is said to them
- Not follow long sentences
- Get tired more easily
- Have difficulty in processing in the additional language
- Even when the input is understood, have difficulty in communicating back in the additional language
- Feel insecure and so 'opt out', deciding not to talk, or even listen, if they feel pressurized.

Teachers therefore need to be sensitive and encourage communicative situations that promote successful language learning through:

- Comprehensible learning situations, ensuring children understand the input
- Contextual support in the form of practical experiences
- Appropriate modelling of language by adults for children to copy
- Opportunities to communicate confidently in the new language
- Motivation through meaningful activities
- Self-confidence through praise
- Stimulating and enjoyable learning situations.
  (adapted from Dulay, Burt and Krashen, 1982)

In this way the additional language learning is made possible through being well planned by the adults and promoted through activities that the children want to do, enjoy doing and so feel relaxed in doing. Young bilingual children, even with a competent level of English, may not always understand many items of vocabulary that appear to be simple. This may be because they have not been introduced to the words or that the meanings may not have been explained to them – young children will probably not ask for explanations!

Bilingual children may not have had sufficient experience with English language and culture to predict likely objects and events. Their performance depends on whether they can identify with the experience in English and can call upon appropriate vocabulary and structure with which to express their understanding. There may be a gap between what can be understood and what can be actively produced. Teachers need to be aware of what special linguistic, cognitive and social skills bilingual children bring with them to the task of making sense of learning. If there are two or more children with the same first language then they should be encouraged to work in both languages. This is not only beneficial for development in both languages, but also aids concept development.

Watch children talking in their first language with their friends or family – do they seem more fluent, are they more animated? These responses need to be brought into the educational setting. Adults need to do more than ask questions; this can result in limited replies. They need to promote meaningful dialogues and conversations. Teachers need to ensure that their conversations with children include input on:

- Appropriate vocabulary (**the key to learning**)
- How to use it in talking and writing (**the key to grammar**)
- What questions to ask (**the key to complex meanings**)
- How to learn (**learning and thinking strategies**).

Early years teachers need to make the most of the fact that children hear and use language in everyday communication. They need to show children how to use language, how to communicate through using dialogue and useful phrases themselves. This is particularly effective when it is done through practical activities. Repetition should be employed as much as possible, but without making the language use stilted – remember:

meaningful communication is the key

Children should not be expected to recreate structures exactly, so focus on them negotiating the meanings and do not worry so much about mistakes. All teachers are language teachers and therefore need to be aware not only of how to promote optimum learning situations, but also be aware of *themselves* as the most important model for language use. The following points promote language as the key to learning. Early years teachers should:

- Be very aware of their own language use
- Show children how to use the language to communicate with others
- Promote specific vocabulary
- Match the language used to activities and experiences
- Give opportunities for children to use, repeat, understand and consolidate vocabulary
- Connect first language to additional languages
- Contextualize learning giving primary experiences, using visual support whenever possible
- Promote learning through play and active experiences
- Interest, excite and get the children actively involved in talking and doing
- Create an atmosphere where children want to participate
- Support learning through practical resources and interaction with other children
- Exploit previously used language – activate children's prior knowledge
- Use oral strategies – talk and interactive questioning
- Integrate speaking and listening to reading and writing
- Use different forms of questioning – closed/open, concrete/abstract
- Consider pace – allow time for children to think, consolidate and translate
- Ensure that children understand before progressing.
  (Adapted from NALDIC, 1999)

THE FOUNDATION STAGE

Children from 3 to 5 years, whether they receive education in nursery schools, reception classes, playgroups, Foundation Stage Units, Children's Centres, or Surestart centres, are in the Foundation Stage and will be receiving the curriculum through a play-based pedagogy. The Curriculum Guidance for the Foundation Stage is statutory and is composed of six areas of learning:

- **Personal, Social and Emotional Development** – creating an ethos which fosters personal, social, moral and spiritual development and promotes independence, self-control, collaboration
- **Communication, Language and Literacy** – talking and learning, multilingualism, the literate environment, stories, storying, meaning-making
- **Mathematical Development** – developing mathematical ideas and concepts, mathematical language and creativity, contexts for numerical and spatial awareness
- **Knowledge and Understanding of the World** – exploring the natural and made world, fostering similarity, difference and change, observing, classifying and investigating the environment
- **Physical Development** – developing physical control, awareness of space and balance, promoting manipulative skills, indoor and outdoor environment
- **Creative Development** – developing imagination, expression of ideas, creativity and feelings in a variety of responses through art, story, music, dance, role-play.
  (*CGFS: QCA, 2000*)

Each of these areas comprises three phases of stepping-stones and early learning goals that children should achieve by the end of the Foundation Stage, broadly equivalent to Level 1 of the National Curriculum. Just as some children will still be progressing towards the early learning goals at the end of the Foundation Stage, some children will achieve and progress beyond them during this stage. The achievement of children beyond the early learning goals can be described using the level descriptors of the National Curriculum (QCA/DfEE, 1999). The Foundation Stage is part of the National Curriculum and it is also linked to the curriculum for children aged 0–3 years – 'Birth to Three Matters'. The National Primary Strategy prioritizes the Foundation Stage, embedding it in all early years settings.

Inclusion for all children is central to the practice and teachers need to 'break down any barriers' to learning, equality and inclusion – no child should be excluded or disadvantaged. Effective early years education requires both a developmentally appropriate curriculum and qualified staff who are knowledgeable about the development and learning of young children. The Foundation Stage curriculum should build upon what children already know and can do, as well as what engages their interest.

PLANNING FOR A DEVELOPMENTALLY APPROPRIATE CURRICULUM FOR THE YOUNG BILINGUAL CHILD

Early years education is built upon giving children practical, first-hand, experiential learning situations. Children work hard at their play – this is what motivates them and helps them learn about the world. Play is both the context and the vehicle that enables them to take ownership of that learning. Teachers provide educational experiences through play in order to engage children's interest, to promote active involvement and encourage learning in both the cognitive and language domains. Resources, activities, situations and experiences are planned for particular learning purposes. Language is the key to developing young bilingual children's understanding, to enable learning to occur, so opportunities for talk are crucial. The objectives that children need to achieve by the end of the Foundation Stage are set out in the early learning goals for *Communication, Language and Literacy*:

- Enjoy listening to and using spoken and written language, and readily turn to it in their play and learning; explore and experiment with sounds, words and texts; listen with enjoyment and respond to stories, songs and other music, rhymes and poems and make up their own stories, songs, rhymes and poems.
- Use language to imagine and recreate roles and experiences.
- Use talk to organize, sequence and clarify thinking, ideas, feelings and events.
- Sustain attentive listening, responding to what they have heard by relevant comments, questions or actions.
- Interact with others, negotiating plans and activities and taking turns in conversation; extend their vocabulary, exploring the meanings and sounds of new words.
- Re-tell narratives in the correct sequence, drawing on the language patterns of stories.
- Speak clearly and audibly with confidence and control and show awareness of the listener, for example by their use of conventions such as greetings, 'please' and 'thank you'.
- Hear and say initial and final sounds in words, and short vowel sounds within words; link sounds to letters, naming and sounding the letters of the alphabet.
- Read a range of familiar and common words and simple sentences independently.
- Know that print carries meaning, and, in English, is read from left to right and top to bottom.
- Show an understanding of the elements of stories, such as main character, sequence of events, and openings, and how information can be found in non-fiction texts to answer questions about where, who, why and how.
- Attempt writing for various purposes, using features of different forms such as lists, stories and instructions.
- Write their own names and other things such as labels and captions and begin to form simple sentences, sometimes using punctuation.
- Use their phonic knowledge to write simple regular words and make phonetically plausible attempts at more complex words.
- Use a pencil and hold it effectively to form recognizable letters, most of which are correctly formed.
  (CGFS: QCA, 2000)

The rest of this chapter will present ideas for promoting speaking and listening to help achieve these objectives.

PROMOTING SPEAKING AND LISTENING IN CIRCLE TIME

Speaking and listening skills need to be developed through promoting communication and cooperation with others, both adults and children. Children learn language best in an environment rich with opportunities that engage them in practical experiences and interaction with significant others and gives them opportunities to explore objects and ideas. To get the meaning of anything, you do not listen only to the individual words, you comprehend them by awareness of the setting or context in which they occur, and that includes the language itself, the topic, the place, who is speaking and even the intonation which the speaker uses. Children need lots of practice in speaking and listening to others. They need lots of experiences to tell real and imagined stories, to explore, develop and clarify ideas and describe events and experiences.

Settings need to provide times when children can be listened to by both other children and adults throughout the day. Teachers should provide many opportunities for children to share and report on what has made them excited – such as a celebration, the arrival of a visitor or new baby, the sharing of a meal – but also whatever made them sad or frightened – a loss, a bereavement, an illness. They need to be encouraged to share home events, to offer accounts of visits, be it to the shops or to a special place of worship. They need to be asked to explain how things work, why things work, what they feel, why they feel. If we as teachers cannot model listening and so show the children how to do so themselves, then how can we ask children to do it? We cannot ask for their respect, if we show them little ourselves. Circle time is an extremely effective way of promoting opportunities for speaking and listening, and stories provide rich contexts. Once children become familiar with well-known stories like *Goldilocks* you can adopt approaches such as:

- Think about what made Baby Bear sad; what would make him happy?
- Think about why Goldilocks ate Baby Bear's porridge.
- Think what Mummy and Daddy Bear should do next.

The adult can provide or model the language through story, using props. This will enable children to gain confidence through repeating the vocabulary and language structures modelled by the adult. Some children may only feel confident saying single-word sentences, but if they can repeat what the adult and the other children have modelled, this can be very supportive. A teacher – in role – can promote supportive 'hot seating' opportunities, examining different versions of similar stories, creating alternative endings, but mainly just by telling stories to which the children not only listen attentively but also participate themselves in the telling.

The children benefit from the teacher's knowledge of their linguistic capabilities and experiences by the way she or he structures the storytelling accordingly. The children listen and feed the language back, and the structures and concepts appear in their stories, told and written – all signs that they have retained the vocabulary of the story. Oral storytelling gives the teacher potential to interact with the children and these group activities can be more dramatic and interesting than reading a book. Here are some examples of how popular books can be used as a basis for these kinds of activities.

- *Elmer* by Bernard McKee. The first story about Elmer the Elephant is one where children can be encouraged to talk about and identify their separateness and so claim their individuality. They learn to be proud of themselves, however different their background might seem to those around them. Children could be encouraged to speak to a large cardboard model of Elmer and to explain to him why it is acceptable to be different and valuable to be yourself. In this way the children are engaged and empowered and able to empathize and articulate. Elmer could be hidden and the children told that he was too shy to speak to them and they can be allowed to search for him and bring him back to the group where he will be affirmed by listening to them, as the children support *his* speaking skills.

- *Farmer Duck* by Martin Waddell. Farmer Duck, unfortunately, lives with a lazy old farmer and has to do all the work. The farmer keeps leaning out of the window and shouting, 'How goes the work?' and the duck replies 'Quack' as he irons, milks the cows, feeds the pigs, washes up, gardens, hoes the turnips. The duck is put under pressure because he has to do all the work, but he has a cunning plan and organizes all the other farm animals to tip the farmer out of bed and the farmer then runs off. The animals then all share the work. This story fulfils the early learning goal of repetition and predictive pattern in story. Encourage the children to empathize with the duck, saying, 'I don't like doing all this work', 'I'm fed up', 'I don't want to do the ironing,' or 'I'm tired.' In this way the children can be moved from repeating single words to longer descriptive sentences. Teaching assistants, nursery nurses and more capable children are positioned at strategic points around the circle, so that the fuller more descriptive sentences are modelled, heard and repeated. The props from the story support the language development and they act as prompts as they are passed round for the children to handle.

Other stories that can be used in this way often contain a chorus or reprise, such as:

- *Owl Babies* by Martin Waddell. The three owl babies have different views about the fact that their mum has disappeared. They have fears and worries with which the children can empathize and go on to share any of their own.

- *The Gruffalo* by Julia Donaldson/Axel Scheffler. The Gruffalo has distinctive features: tusks, teeth, purple spines, large green eyes. Children can name all the animals: mouse, snake, fox etc. There's a useful moral for PSHE – 'don't believe everything you are told'.

- *The Rainbow Fish* by Marcus Psister. This is the story of the beautiful rainbow fish who will at first not share his glistening scales and so is lonely without friends. Then he takes advice and learns to share a little of himself with others. The children in the group need to ask for a scale and say why they want it and what they will do with it.

All these stories promote diversity and can be used to support individual needs and equality. The children need then to be moved towards offering their own ideas. The following phrases are examples of sentence stems that can support children's speaking in turn at circle time. The teacher models the sentence stem and adds an ending. The children may at first just repeat the same sentence, but with encouragement will soon begin to think of different ideas. It also needs to be remembered that all of these activities can be done in a range of different languages:

- Ap ka nam kya heh. Mera nam ... heh. *(What's your name? My name is ...)*
- Qui s'appelle ... Je m'appelle ... *(Who's called ...? I'm called ...)*
- I like it when ...
- My friend is ...
- Because ...
- I am good at ...
- At school ...
- The weather today is ...
- This is my finger. These are my toes.
- Who put the cookie in the cookie jar?

CONTEXTUALIZING SPEAKING AND LISTENING – PRACTICAL IDEAS FOR RESOURCING

The 'communicative' experiences introduced in circle time need to be developed throughout the day through all the activities happening in the setting. There needs to be a plethora of opportunities for the children to talk, not only with an adult, but also by themselves in pairs or in small groups. The adults need to be strategic, offering support, extra vocabulary and sentence stems at appropriate times. Try to provide this support by becoming actively involved without interrupting and inhibiting the children's play. For real understanding to occur it should be firmly rooted in practical experiences that connect the language and conceptual development. We will look at three ways in which language-rich play can be promoted:

- Theme trays
- Storysacks
- Topics

Theme trays

Teachers in the Foundation Stage Unit and KS1 at Carlton School in Dewsbury extolled the value of using theme trays with their young bilingual children. Theme trays are collections of resources which can be played with, based on a theme. They are placed in a 'builder's tray' – a large, black, rigid, one metre-square tray. A base play mat can be positioned in the tray, which has a picture landscape of the environment of the theme.

Key questions posed by the adults will support the problem-solving processes and allow imaginative play to be developed along with language. These can be scripted for any adults to help them achieve and clarify the language and activity objectives. These support children's speaking and listening skills and are also an important part of the observation and assessment process in determining what level each child is working at and his or her performance in first and additional language. The adult can then rephrase the language to meet an individual child's language capability.

Supporting speaking and listening through small-world role play; extension of language; learning from one another through play without having to do a whole topic – much can be covered through incidental experiential play. Adults can read books and help children to discover more about the theme. Vocabulary development should be promoted in an ongoing and purposeful way. Here are five of Carlton's most successful theme trays.

Builder's Yard

Different vehicles – tipper trucks, cement wagons, lorries – and miniature world people with a range of accessories – builders' hats, spades, tabards, coats, wheelbarrows and signs saying: *Beware, Keep Left, Keep Right, Give Way* etc. The tray is filled with gravel and sand so that the children can transport the materials in the vehicles, make roadways and engage in social and problem solving play. Information books about trucks and building, and storybooks such as *Bob the Builder* are available for the children to access, get ideas from and begin to read and interpret the language. There is one child-sized hard hat so that one child is in charge of the role play. Adults can prompt problems and tasks by asking questions such as:

- What materials do you need for the houses?
- How will you move the materials?
- What is the purpose of this vehicle?
- What do you think this is for?

Minibeasts

This is a very common theme that is explored in Foundation Stage classes in the spring and summer months when children are able to explore the outdoor environment more often. For this theme the identification of the minibeasts is a key and the promotion of their names, number of legs, attributes, characteristics, life cycles, movements can be explored. Even quite complicated vocabulary such as *antennae, proboscis* and *arachnid* can be promoted when linked to actual objects or characteristics. Action verbs such as *crawling, flying, scampering, slithering* can be used to promote both the small-world play and physical development. All the minibeasts – and also mosses, lichens, grasses, wood, rocks, pebbles, stones, mud, bark, soil – can assure the children that 'soil is not muck!'. There is quite a lot of poetry available about minibeasts. Positioning language – *up, over, under, beside* – is naturally developed. Some questions to ask are:

- What does this insect need to survive?
- Where would it like to live?
- In what ways are the insects different?

Jungle

Lots of little plastic trees and rocks, including a huge rock with holes and ledges for animals to be positioned at different levels, create the jungle environment. There should be large and small jungle animals. Natural materials should be added – ferns, grasses, twigs and leaves – these can be placed in playdough or Blu-tack® so that they can stand upright or be firmly positioned by the children. Language is developed through naming the animals, talking about size, labelling families – babies, mothers, fathers. Some questions to ask are:

- What does this animal need to live?
- Where would it like to be?
- In what ways are the animals different?

Antarctic

First, it must be remembered that penguins and polar bears do not live at the same pole. Penguins live at the Antarctic, polar bears do not. This is a very tactile theme tray. Children recreate the scene through glass beads, fabric, cotton wool, collage materials, glass pebbles, fabric, net. The penguins are of different sizes. Fiction and information books are available to discover how a penguin lives. The Antarctic is an unlikely topic for the Foundation Stage, so this theme tray is an ideal opportunity for children to explore something new and different. Some questions to ask are:

- What does this animal need to live?
- Where would it like to be?
- In what ways are the animals different?

Seashore

This theme is based on a story in rhyme – *Commotion in the Ocean* by Giles Andreae. This offers a different dimension for the children and introduces rhyme and rhythm, which really supports children's language as they learn through the cues and repetition that the poetic story offers. Use tapes of sea sounds, seabirds crying, waves, foghorns; as sea songs can help provide an atmosphere. This is a really inexpensive theme tray to develop, as one just needs to spend a day as a beachcomber collecting mussel, whelk, winkle and cockle shells, crab shells, dried seaweed, driftwood, fishing net floats, all of which are freely found on beaches. This is also a very tactile theme with the handling of the shells and sand etc. Builder's silver sand is just like sand found on seashores, or sand available from large DIY stores can be used – it is useful to have sand of different textures and colours, wet and dry sand. The children themselves can add the water and experiment with changing the consistency of the dry sand. Some questions to ask are:

- What textures are there?
- What sounds can you hear?
- What could be happening?

Storysacks

Stories work with all children, but in particular with bilingual learners. It is very important to model the story, for the adults working with the children to role play the Billy Goat, the Giant, Baby Bear. If we don't demonstrate, how can we expect the children to learn? An important tool is to 'shadow tell' the story; when the children are in role, offer them the words to repeat and they will expand upon these when they become confident. Reading stories is fine, telling is fine, but neither of these are enough for children to become confident in using the words and phrases.

Storysacks were the brainwave of Neil Griffiths. Many schools are now using storysacks that they have either made with parents or bought from commercial suppliers. Try to ensure that you provide a range of stories from different cultures and backgrounds. At all points, be aware of the need to both affirm and extend the children – provide stories that they can see themselves in and stories that take them into environments other than their own. The following stories are suitable ones with which to provide accompanying storysacks. Many of these stories have repetitive language that enables the children to tell the story easily whilst handling the characters and props:

- *Red Riding Hood* and other traditional tales
- *The Very Hungry Caterpillar*
- *Handa's Surprise*
- *Stone Soup*
- *Topiwalo the Hatmaker*
- *Mrs Wishy Washy*
- *Where the Wild Things Are*
- *Mr Gumpy's Outing*
- *Sandeep and the Parrots*
- *Send for Sohail!*

Then Haruna had a problem. "There's a tiger in my classroom," she said. "My teacher is sitting on top of the cupboard and he's too frightened to come down."

All the children in the playground knew what to do. They all said immediately...

"Send for Sohail!"

Now whenever Sohail was sent for, he always came, quick as a flash.

"A tiger," he remarked . "That's only a small problem. Didn't you know that tigers love milk?" and he went to the milkman and got thirty bottles of milk.

"Come on tiger," he shouted, as he poured all the milk into a dustbin lid. The tiger looked wary, but very slowly came out and had a big, big drink. Then before the tiger could blink, Sohail slipped a skipping-rope around his neck and took him back to the zoo.

خدا کی بُول لگے۔

بَیٹل کی اُلّو!

Figure 3.1 From *Send for Sohail!* (reproduced by permission of Partnership Publishing ©1993)

Here are some examples of modelling language through story using *Send for Sohail!* This was a story written by the children at Grange Road First School with their teacher Maggie Power, illustrated by a student artist and published by Bradford College. It is a story modelled on the popular *Happy Families* series by Janet and Allan Ahlberg, telling the story of the brave and bold Sohail, who came to the rescue when various disasters threatened the neighbourhood. The pictures are colourful and lively, and the text is presented with English and Urdu side by side on the page (see Figure 3.1). (Details of how to obtain copies are given at the end of Chapter 5.)

The teacher can share the telling through choosing children to be Sohail and other characters and offering the words for them to copy. In this way the teacher gets children involved in a joint participation and telling of the story. The children can use the same words as the teacher, which can then be used again in a retelling using story props. This is then followed by getting the children to tell the story with pictures, which can then be rearranged and retold again. The children can make the 'still images' in the picture come to life and create a scene, if they are given sentences with which to work. For example:

- 'Send for Sohail!'.
- 'When you want some help. Send for Sohail!'
- 'There's a tiger in the room. Send for Sohail!'
- 'My teacher's frightened of mice. Send for Sohail!'
- 'Oh, I'm an elephant. I'm frightened of mice. Send for Sohail!'
- 'I'm Sohail, I've come to help.'

In this way the teacher offers and models the language the children need. The children join in, repeat the words and copy the sentence structures. They will very quickly make up their own sentences, which can become more elaborate as they progress. The children will share their stories with one another and begin to read and retell by themselves and in groups. All this can be done in any language.

Topics

Topics and themes as a way of promoting learning are now again gaining priority in early years and KS1 classrooms. Young children's learning is not compartmentalized into separate subjects. They need to make links and connect new learning to previous knowledge and experience. Topics are very useful vehicles to carry the learning and help children make connections. Sometimes it is not the knowledge that is important, as much as the key skills and concepts that need to be introduced again and again to young children for them to be embedded in their understanding. Their knowledge and understanding normally depend on the amount of experiences they have had before arriving in a Foundation Stage setting. Colour, size, shape and number are key concepts that may need lots of repetition for some young children. The six areas of learning, the early learning goals and the stepping stones can be delivered through cross-curricular learning through relevant topics or themes. The following suggestions are common topics or themes in the early years. They can all be planned and delivered in a way that provides multicultural experiences, exploring similarities and differences, using a range of resources that promote a variety of cultural experiences:

- Precious Things
- The Senses
- All about Me
- Food

- Transport
- Minibeasts
- Materials
- Weather
- Pets
- Toys
- Buildings
- Harvest
- Clothes

CONCLUSION

All of the ideas described here are valuable, but to get full benefit from any and all of them, they need to be modelled. There needs to be the scaffolding in place, so that the children's language is being valued first and then enriched. As well as supporting and developing children's language, first and additional, it must be remembered that all of us have learnt through play. These activities should stimulate children. They can provide enrichment and enjoyment for all and also make their way into homes, so that parents and families can help model the language promoted through these activities.

A young mother shared with us the story of her child, who, when she had just come home from school, arranged her toys in front of a big book and then, using her wooden spoon to point, indicated the value of using full stops to her teddies and dolls! Of equal importance was the need for her to convey the value she felt in being special.

Summary: Key principles for promoting children's learning in the early years

- Support in the first language develops self-confidence and forms links with prior learning experiences.
- The Foundation Stage framework allows opportunities for the use of first language in children's learning.
- Children in the early years need a full range of hands-on, contextualized learning experiences to promote learning.
- Stories provide an excellent vehicle for allowing children to talk about home and family experiences.
- A range of resources, topics and themes is needed to provide opportunities for contextualized, meaningful talk, which is essential for learning.

FURTHER READING

Dulay, Heidi, Burt, Marina and Krashen, Stephen (1982) *Language Two*. Oxford: Oxford University Press.

NALDIC (National Association for Language Development in the Curriculum) (1999) *The Distinctiveness of English as an Additional Language: A Cross-curriculum Discipline*. Working Paper 5.

QCA (2000) *Curriculum Guidance for the Foundation Stage*. London: DfEE. Available at www.qca.org.uk.

Chapter 4

Talking, Learning and Moving on to Writing

Jean Conteh, Shirley Davids and Kathryn Bownass

This chapter is about the importance of talk in bilingual children's learning and ways of promoting talk in primary classrooms. It also discusses moving on from purposeful talk to meaningful writing.

For many bilingual pupils, learning English goes hand-in-hand with learning new concepts in different subjects across the curriculum, so talk is important in two main ways:

- As a means of developing children's skills and knowledge in English
- To support the learning of new concepts and ideas in all subjects across the curriculum.

In other words, while bilingual pupils are:

learning to talk in English.

They are also:

talking to learn.

Bilingual learners, like all learners in primary school, need plenty of opportunities to talk in interesting, purposeful and increasingly complex ways. Just as they need guidance in developing their skills in reading and writing, they need guidance in developing their skills in speaking and listening.

One way in which opportunities for talk can be provided, both within the framework of the Literacy Hour and in activities in other areas of the curriculum, is through promoting collaborative talk in the classroom. In the next section, we explain what we mean by collaborative talk. After this, we describe two projects that were successful in providing opportunities for helping children to talk collaboratively, purposefully and meaningfully, and then move on to produce powerful writing. The first is about using debates and the second about using role play based on the *Pandora's Box* story.

COLLABORATIVE TALK

What is it?

Collaborative talk is the kind of classroom talk that encourages children to become actively engaged in their learning. It can take place in any subject area, not just the Literacy Hour or other English lessons. It has three main purposes:

- It helps children to learn specific new words, phrases and grammar in English, related to the topics under discussion, in rich and meaningful ways.
- It helps you as a teacher to ensure that your pupils fully understand the concepts you want to teach them.
- It helps develop children's confidence to take part in structured discussions and conversations for specific purposes, and so further enhance their learning.

In different activities, one or more of these purposes will be the main focus.

Why is collaborative talk important?

Collaborative talk promotes children's learning in the three main ways that were discussed in Chapter 1:

- By providing opportunities for 'rich scripting' to develop
- By contextualizing learning in concrete experiences
- By scaffolding as children move from concrete to abstract activity, thinking and use of language.

Rich scripting

Collaborative talk provides a framework in which the teacher can introduce new technical and academic language connected with the subject being learnt. Through the talk, the new vocabulary can be revisited many times. This is important for all children, but especially for bilingual children, because it means they will meet new words more than once in different phrases and sentences, so their understanding of the words will grow and develop; their meanings for the words will be much richer than if they were simply given short definitions at the start of the activity. So, their understanding of the academic subjects they are learning will develop in a much richer way than if they were being presented with simplified vocabulary, orally or on worksheets. Their knowledge of English and their confidence will improve as they use the language in active and practical ways, and their conceptual learning will also be strengthened.

Contextualizing learning

Through collaborative talk, we are helping to base children's learning in concrete, contextualized experience, as explained in Chapter 1. In your planning, try to build the following three stages into each activity, so that you help to make sure that your pupils' learning is well grounded in a supportive context:

1. Let children begin by talking about things in the 'here and now', embedded in the immediate context, focused on a hands-on experience.
2. Gradually move children to talking about what they are doing in ways not connected with the immediate, 'hands-on' actions, e.g. through recounting or reporting what they have done.
3. Then move them on to talking and writing about what they have done in more formal academic ways.

Scaffolding

As their learning progresses through the three stages shown above, children are moving from concrete to a more abstract academic level of meaning in their use of language. With support, their language is progressively becoming disembedded from the context in which it is occurring, and their meanings are conveyed in the language itself, not in any surrounding activity or resources. As this develops, they are ready to engage in meaningful, purposeful writing. As we emphasize throughout this book, this move from *embedded* to *disembedded* language is very important for bilingual children's learning. Indeed, all children need support as they develop the skills that enable them to use language in this way.

SOME GUIDELINES FOR PROMOTING COLLABORATIVE TALK

Collaborative talk fits in well in both the Literacy and Numeracy Hours as well as in other subjects in the curriculum; it can be part of whole-class input, groupwork or plenaries. In collaborative talk, active *listening* is just as important as *speaking*. Both speaker and listener are actively working, though only one will be speaking at a time. At first, taking part in collaborative discussions will not come naturally to most children. Teachers need to model this kind of talk, just as you might model a particular kind of writing or reading for your pupils. Collaborative talk can happen in whole-class, group or one-to-one settings – the important thing is the way the activity is planned in order to support the talk.

Getting started

You will need to provide clear guidelines for your pupils, explaining how you want them to behave, both as speakers and listeners. The best way to begin is to model for them, giving them the chance to listen to an authentic discussion taking place, perhaps between you and another adult. Explain to them what you are doing, and why, and – as you go on – ask questions in order to include your pupils in the discussion.

It is also helpful to give the children a realistic example of discussion, for example you could show them a short extract of a TV debate or interview on a relevant topic. Ask them to watch and listen carefully, and encourage them to identify words or phrases that they think are especially useful in the discussion. They could note these words and phrases down and compare them afterwards with those that other children have written. Emphasize the importance of the different roles that speakers and listeners play in the interview or debate, and your pupils will quickly follow the model and start to adopt the more 'grown up' forms of speech they hear.

Once pupils have had the experience of hearing collaborative talk in this way, they can begin to practise it with their peers in small groups. At this stage, you could allow pupils to work in groups with others who share the same home languages. They can be encouraged to use the languages with which they feel most comfortable to discuss with one another, then they will report back to you or the rest of the class in English.

A classroom ethos to support collaboration

It is very important to develop the kind of classroom ethos which will support collaborative talk and help children to see that what they are doing is just as serious as writing or reading. If they pick up the message that it is not really an important part of the lesson, or that they are not expected to make serious contributions to the conversation, children will not participate to the best of their ability. If they believe the activity is serious and they know why they are doing it, then they will participate with full seriousness.

Wells and Chang-Wells (1992) offer guidance for teachers on how to develop the kind of classroom ethos that will promote collaborative talk with their pupils. They describe a set of actions teachers can take, and call this *leading from behind*. Here is a summary of their main points:

- Always take seriously what children say.
- Listen carefully to what children say and ask them specific questions to help you to understand fully the points they want to make.
- When you respond, try to extend and develop what children say, and encourage them to do this themselves.
- Try to take account of what you know of each individual child's strengths and needs in your responses – treat each child as a serious conversation partner.
- While keeping your learning objectives in mind, try to modify your responses in the light of what children say.

As you can see, these guidelines contain important messages for planning and working. You need to have clear learning goals and structures for your lessons. But you also need the confidence to be flexible about the ways in which you achieve these goals with your pupils. This can take time to establish so that you and your pupils feel comfortable and secure.

This does *not* mean you are expected to adopt a totally new way of working, but rather a new approach to the way talk is managed and developed in your classroom. An important first step in initiating this approach is for you to share your intentions with your class. Based on the points made by Wells and Chang-Wells, you could develop some guidelines for collaborative talk in discussion with your pupils. You could agree some ground rules to be used in whole-class, group or one-to-one discussion situations. The rules could then be displayed on a poster and referred to regularly as your pupils become more familiar with these ways of talking and working.

We will now look in detail at a project that has proved successful in helping children to talk collaboratively. In the next section, Shirley Davids describes her work with Year 6 pupils using debates.

PROJECT 1: PROMOTING COLLABORATIVE TALK THROUGH DEBATES

'Man U are great, Miss.'
'Do you think so? Why, what makes them so good?'
'I dunno, miss. They just are.'

How often do we get such a response from our pupils? From children who struggle to articulate even the most basic needs, emotions and feelings, who cannot offer original opinions, arguments or ideas? The problem seems to affect many children today, whether bilingual or monolingual. Yet the Primary National Strategy urges that we teach children to:

- Participate in whole class debates …
- Handle relevant questions from an audience …
- Attract and hold the listeners' attention through what is said and how it is delivered …
  (*Objective 62, Speaking listening and learning: working with children from KS1 and 2,* DES, 2003)

and when writing, to:

- Construct an effective argument
- Develop a point logically and effectively
- Anticipate objections
- Illustrate points persuasively.
  (*NLS text objectives 15 and 18: Year 6 Term 2*)

The task can seem a daunting one, especially to teachers of pupils who have only been learning English since starting school. How can we guide our pupils to offer their ideas, to speak from the heart, say what they mean?

A few years ago, by accident, I opened a door that gave me access to ways to provide each child a voice with which to speak their thoughts. This door was the use of debates in lessons.

'The school I was working in, a Church of England Primary with almost 98% bilingual children, was at the time promoting speaking and listening as a tool for learning. I set aside 15 minutes at the end of a lesson to introduce the idea of debates. It was an informal "see how they cope" session to form a basis for future planning. I was blessed at the time with a classroom assistant who had previously taught A-level English in a secondary school. After introducing the topic, giving the children a few minutes to jot down ideas, then choosing two suitable pupils to make the first speeches, I asked Mrs D. to introduce the debate formally. Completely off the cuff, she adopted a 'posh' accent, a very formal tone and used traditional phrases and terminology. The children were spellbound. Within minutes, they were all offering contributions, arguing, sparring,

(Continued)

conceding points. They were hooked. I circulated, prompted the hesitant, played devil's advocate and tried to keep the proceedings in order.

The children had quickly realized we were acting – for real! It was a game they could join in. They enjoyed every minute of it, and would have talked on through break, dinner or home time, given the chance. The floodgates were opened. It became apparent that the very formal setting and the ground rules we established in that first trial run were an important key, as was the choice of topic for discussion. However, we had found in debates a tool that empowered all our children to speak with passion and conviction on a range of topics. The next step was to build in the language structures and key skills to make these sessions valuable across the curriculum.'

Most of our debates follow the pattern outlined below, adapted to suit the age, experience and confidence of the class.

Outline of a typical debate

This kind of debate can be planned as part of a lesson in different curriculum areas. It is particularly suited to History or Geography, but could equally well be part of an activity in Science, RE or other curriculum area.

Before the debate

- The teacher suggests the motion, but does not discuss it. It should be a topic which the children have been learning something about, so that they have some knowledge of the issues.
- The children spend 10 minutes individually writing their initial reactions.
- The teacher chooses a chairperson – a confident member of the class to begin with, then others later when they have some experience.
- The teacher chooses speakers – at first one for each 'side', later two of each (it helps to begin with confident children with plenty to say for themselves, who will provide a model for others in later sessions).

The chairperson's role

The first time you organize a debate, use a classroom assistant or other adult as chair if possible, then teach the role to a child – they need to be able to handle the others confidently. Eventually, the children will be able to run the whole thing themselves. You can then step back, listen, direct and observe from the wings, literally 'lead from behind', watch the performance develop and listen closely, taking note of points to praise the children on afterwards, and also teaching points for future lessons.

Providing a prompt sheet for the chairperson is a good way to give moral support and also ensure they have access to the kind of language they need to fulfil their role. A photocopiable prompt sheet is given on the next page.

Chairperson's Prompt Sheet for Debates

Good morning and welcome to our debate held today at ...

The motion today is ...

First I would like to welcome our speakers.

Proposing the motion is ... , famous for his work in ...

The seconder of the motion, ... is well known as ...

Speaking against the motion are ... and ...

Thank you for your contributions, I would like to open the debate to the floor, who would like to comment?

Thank you sir, the gentleman at the rear of the hall, wearing glasses, ...

A good/interesting/valid point, thank you.

Madam, the lady at the front in yellow ...

I wonder if our speaker for the motion would like to comment/answer that point ...

The last contribution from the floor now ... thank you.

I will now take a vote on the motion.

Would those in favour please raise their hands – and those against – any abstentions?

I declare the motion carried/defeated. This house believes ...

During the debate

- The chairperson and four speakers take up their seats at the front of the room.
- The teacher plays 'TV announcer' and introduces the programme.
- The chairperson welcomes the audience, announces the motion, and introduces the speakers.
- The speakers for the motion give their views, each speaking for 2–3 minutes, followed by the speakers against the motion.
- The chairperson opens the debate to the floor, inviting speakers one at a time – speakers can only join in at the invitation of the chairperson, or when directly questioned by the audience.
- When the time limit is approaching, the chairperson thanks speakers and audience and summarizes the main points of the debate.
- The chairperson then asks for a vote, including abstentions.
- The chairperson announces the result of the vote and formally closes the debate.

Notice the formal language expected of the chairperson – this is one of the keys to a successful debate. If all the children who take part are encouraged to speak in this way, it remainds them that they are involved in a serious task, and they must behave accordingly.

Debates in the Literacy Hour

The more you use debates with your pupils, the more skilled they will become as debaters, and the more language they will learn. A range of learning outcomes can be met in debates; many from the Literacy Strategy are not subject-specific, so could also be built into activities across the curriculum once the basic skills and routines are mastered. For example, in History a debate could be, 'What have the Greeks done for us?' or in Geography, 'Should we build the motorway here?'. This is another very good way of contextualizing learning in activities that will be meaningful for pupils.

As well as using a debate in different curriculum areas as a means of teaching new language and new concepts, you can use the Literacy Hour time to set up a full and formal debate, planning into it specific language objectives from the strategy framework. The box shows some Literacy Hour objectives that can be met in debates.

Year 3, Term 3, text 5 Year 3, Term 3, text 22	Discuss characters, feelings, behaviour, relationships Experiment with recounting the same event in a variety of ways
Year 4, Term 3, text 21 Year 4, Term 3, text 23	Assemble and sequence points in order to plan the presentation of points of view Present a point of view in writing
Year 5, Term 3, text 17 Year 5, Term 4, text 19	Draft and write a letter to put a point of view Construct an argument in note form or full text to persuade others

(Continued)

(Continued)

Year 6, Term 1, text 15	Develop a journalistic style through considering balanced and ethical reporting
Year 6, Term 2, text 18	Construct effective arguments, develop a point logically and effectively, support and illustrate points persuasively

Guidelines for developing debates as part of focused literacy activities

1. Choose a suitable topic – something you and your pupils will want to talk about, something relevant to everyday life, topical and interesting. Some of the topics that have been used successfully are given below.
2. Aim high. The children will have views on a variety of complex topics. Be confident enough to handle whatever arises and actively demonstrate respect for the children's views to give them the security to voice their ideas.
3. Offer children a variety of roles to adopt. They should also be able to invent their own. As they gain confidence, they can change roles mid-debate, and offer a contrasting point of view. It's useful to have one or two authority figures (a policeman is always popular especially with the 'naughty' boys) or a teacher, headteacher, local MP, nurse, doctor, shopkeeper, parent or grandparent. It's good to have a 'baddie' or two, such as a criminal or a 'lager lout' (the well-behaved children like adopting this role to try it out!).
4. The role of 'non-English speaker' can be popular – or limited-English speaker. The child brave enough to try this option is to be welcomed, along with their 'interpreter'.
5. Once a motion has been adopted, give children a maximum of 10 minutes to scribble ideas, in pairs, groups or alone if they are more comfortable. Allow children to make notes in the language they feel most comfortable using. Members of the floor should make notes as well, so that they are ready to contribute with questions.
6. Stick to the script or rules of formal debates (see above). This provides a safe, secure place from which to argue. It's like a stage, or court room.

Follow the rules yourself – for example, put your hand up if you want to offer opinions, don't call out and over-ride what is happening, and so on.

Here are some topics which we have used successfully in debates:

- This house believes our school uniform is completely unsuitable for daily life in school.
- This house believes that all people who come to live in the UK should take a test in English before arrival.
- This house believes that scarves should not be worn in school, as they are a sign of religious belief (following from the French ruling on religious symbols in schools).
- This house believes that homework is unnecessary, indeed harmful to a child's well-being.
- This house believes that school dinners should be phased out.

- This house believes that taking a pen or paper from school for personal use at home is stealing.
- This house believes that the road outside school should be closed to traffic.

Planning a debate in the Literacy Hour

The sections of the Literacy Hour lend themselves to language work that helps to prepare children for taking part in a debate. Here are some suggestions for things you can do in the different stages of the hour.

Word work   This is a good opportunity to introduce some of the more technical language to be used in the debate by looking at root words and their meanings. It also gives the opportunity to develop the children's ability to use different prefixes/suffixes in context. Choose a set of words that are relevant, for example the school dinners debate lends itself to using *diet, dieting, dietician, nutrients, nutrition, nutritious.* Typical questions could be:

- What is the meaning and origin of *nutrient*?
- Can you use the different word forms correctly in sentences?
- What are the two ways of using *diet*?
- Can you spell the words?

Sentence work   The words introduced at the start of the lesson can now be used in sentences (using whatever grammatical point is currently being taught). This is an opportunity to practise use of vocabulary and sentence structure in a meaningful way. For example, if teaching the use of commas in clauses, model a sentence using a clause, such as:

> *School dinners, which are cooked from fresh ingredients,*
> *are an excellent source of nutrients.*

The children can then work in pairs to develop their own sentences starting with *School dinners, which ... , are ...* Points can be scored for use of the day's new words. The children can try out their ideas with a partner, without being overheard. When they have a suitable example ready, they can offer it to the class. Technical and formal language is quickly adopted using this format and the more able children quickly see the opportunity for humour. Here is an example, that one child came up with from the model above:

> *School dinners, which are prepared with fresh sprouts and cabbage,*
> *are frequently left uneaten despite being extremely nutritious.*

Shared text   Initially, the spoken word is the key and children should have plenty of time to hear and practise speaking the kinds of language needed in debates. Then, there is usually a suitable text available on the subject to be discussed, in the form of a letter to the newspaper, a magazine article, leaflet or similar publication. All of these kinds of text are very useful, as they are all written in the kinds of language used to argue and persuade, which is particularly relevant for debates. The chosen text can be used to obtain examples of vocabulary, punctuation, grammar or general viewpoints, when the writing stage is reached.

An example plan for a debate lesson in the Literacy Hour

The lesson described below was actually used as a revision session just prior to SATs week. The topic allowed full use of the vocabulary introduced in word work, and the language structures and phrases modelled in sentence work were also tried out. The ideas introduced in work on Ancient Greek civilizations in history were brought into focus. For revision, it allowed persuasive techniques to be revisited and a whole range of viewpoints to be aired.

Times are given for each stage of the activity, to fit into an hour, but remember that you can be flexible and adjust times to suit the pace of working which best suits your pupils.

Activity: Debate lesson plan – 'Who writes the rules?'

Learning objectives

- To use a range of oral techniques to present persuasive arguments
- To speak for different audiences, use conventions of formal debates
- To construct a logical argument
- To hold an audience's attention (gesture, eye contact)
- To speak in role/from own point of view

Word work – 5 mins

Vocabulary development – Dictionary work in groups or pairs

Teacher writes on the board:

civic, polis, city

Ask questions that can be answered from the dictionaries:

- What are the meanings of these words?
- What other words come from these roots? *(e.g. civilized, civil, civilian)*
- How are the words linked?
- What are their origins? *(Can they spot links to Greek /Latin?)*

In pairs, think of sentences that use civilization, politician, etc.

Add to class list of words spelt with *c* but sound like *s*.

Sentence work – 10 mins

Class session – oral

Teacher models target sentence structure on board:

> … *In my opinion, brussels sprouts are full of nutrients and easy to eat and cheap.* …

or

Chocolate is full of sugar and bad for your health and expensive and bad for your teeth and should never be eaten by children.

In pairs, children are asked to improve these sentences – they are given a few minutes to talk collaboratively in pairs.

Children suggest ways to 'up the level' – i.e. improve the connectives – teacher has several ready on card to prompt (see p. 55). More advanced groups could extend the sentences by adding connectives to contrast ideas, then adding their own ideas which oppose the ones given in the original sentence, e.g.

[Although in your opinion ... I still believe ...]

Again, children try out ideas first for a few minutes in pairs, then share with class.

Shared text work – 10 mins

Text: Martin Luther King's speech on his acceptance of the Nobel Prize in 1963 (slightly adapted):

I have a dream that one day the State of Alabama will be transformed into a situation where little black boys and little black girls will be able to join hands with little white boys and little white girls and walk together as sisters and brothers. I have a dream today. I have a dream that one day every valley shall be exalted, every hill and mountain shall be made low, the rough places will be made plain, and the crooked places will be made straight, and the glory of God shall be revealed, and all flesh shall see it together. This is our hope. This is the faith with which I return to the South. With this faith we will be able to hew out of the mountain of despair a stone of hope. With this faith we will be able to transform the jangling discord of our nation into a beautiful symphony of brotherhood. With this faith we will be able to work together, to pray together, to struggle together, to go to jail together, to stand up for freedom together, knowing that we will one day be free.

[Note for teachers: Martin Luther King's speeches are easily accessed on the internet; one good website is: http://www.mecca.org/~crights/dream.html]

The teacher reads the text, each child has a paper copy on which to highlight features of persuasive writing. Once the reading is finished, children in pairs compare the features of persuasive writing they have spotted.

- repetition
- strong beginning and end
- short sentences for dramatic effect
- 'list' style sentences
- strong, positive language
- links between sentence starts/earlier statements

- alliteration
- facts
- evidence
- quotations

Now we move to the formal debate.

The debate

The motion is:

> *This house believes that children should write the school's rules,*
> *as children are in the majority.*

Independent work – 30 mins

For 10 minutes the whole class, working as individuals/pairs, jot down ideas in draft form, using any language, assuming any role in the debate.

Remind children of language devices that improve persuasive writing (from the speech).

Then, allot roles: chairperson, speakers for and against – police officer, headteacher, parent, child, teacher etc.

For 20 minutes, conduct the actual debate – the children should take the lead.

As 'Master of Ceremonies', the teacher welcomes the audience, then introduces the chairperson, who reads the motion and introduces the speakers before conducting the debate.

Children acting as the audience from the floor can be encouraged to clap politely, say 'hear, hear' and so on to support points they agree with. (This often has the effect of making the speaker visibly 'grow' a few inches!)

Make notes while the speakers are delivering their speeches, to make sure the main points are not forgotten.

Plenary – 5 mins

The chairperson sums up the main points (with the aid of the teacher, who has made notes).

The teacher points out the successful use of structures and vocabulary in the speeches and questions, then gives rewards!

A few closing questions then round off the lesson and the debate:

- Has anyone changed their minds, thought again about this after hearing speeches? Who made you reconsider? Why?
- Which 'side' got more votes? Why?

Prompt sheet for connective words

Connectives to add ideas:

Furthermore

Moreover

Another feature

In addition

Also

Finally

Lastly

Connectives to contrast ideas:

Even though I can see your point that

Nevertheless, I still believe

Despite your view that

Another view would be that

Whilst I respect your view

Although I understand your opinion

Another view would be

Other useful phrases:

I believe

My main point is

I suggest that

If ... then ...

Speaking as a parent

How would you feel if

● **Moving on to writing**

In subsequent Literacy Hour sessions, pupils can go on to do some persuasive writing around the topic. Having heard, argued against and voiced a wide range of opinions in the lesson, children are keen to follow a debate by writing down their thoughts. However, they need structure and organization to help them sort out their ideas.

The simple plan/prompt sheet on the opposite page is useful to get children started in their writing. We then go on to look at a project that helps lead children into more purposeful writing.

Prompt sheet for starting writing

Introduction

Write the question in your own words.

Outline briefly two opposite views, such as:
Whilst some people believe, ... others say that ...

Define any technical words.

Paragraph 1

Points for the motion – main one first then less important ones.
(At least one sentence for each point.)

The main argument:
Many people have said ...

Extension – say why – back it up with evidence:
this is because ...

Paragraph 2

Points against the motion – main one first then less important one.
(As above)
On the other hand ... another argument ... despite this ...
others believe ...

Conclusion

In conclusion, I think that ... because ... I also think that ... Despite ...

PROJECT 2: PANDORA'S BOX: ROLE PLAY INTO WRITING

Many children, even in Year 6, are not very confident when writing about feelings (their own or others'). A good way to overcome this is to use drama techniques which depend on extended, collaborative talk. This enables the children to put themselves in the position of a character in a story, make decisions for the character and also understand the consequences of their actions. Through this, they talk naturally about feelings without self-consciousness or embarrassment.

The main aim of the work described here was to lead the children into meaningful and purposeful writing. The work was based on the *Pandora's Box* story. The opportunity to discuss the ideas and feelings of characters in the story generated powerful language and fed the writing. The story is easily available on the Internet – here are two useful websites:

http://www.physics.hku.hk/~tboyce/ss/topics/prometheus.html
http://www.colum.edu/centers/bpa/epicenter/pandora/themyth.html

In the oral activity, the well-known drama techniques of *conscience alley* and *role play* were used, and proved very successful in generating focused, purposeful talk.

The lesson plan for a Pandora's Box activity is presented below.

Activity: Pandora's Box lesson plan

Learning objectives

- Speaking and Listening: to improvise using a range of drama strategies and conventions to explore themes such as hopes, fears, desires, e.g. drawing on a shared text to explore emotional tension at key moments in a story.
- Curriculum: NLS Year 6, Term 2 text level objectives – narrative

Introduce Pandora's Box

Introduce the topic with discussion about a concrete example of decision-making that the children may have experienced themselves. Discuss why the decisions are so difficult to make.

Read the first part of *Pandora's Box* up to the point where she has to make the decision of whether she will open the box or not.

As a class, discuss the ideas the children have about whether she should open the box or not.

Arrange the children in a circle (allow friendship pairs if the children are not used to doing this – otherwise it could be a quiet session!). Introduce the children to the box (this could be an actual object or you could allow the children to use their imagination). For the session described here, a jewellery box was used.

Ask a few children to come up in turn as Pandora and describe how they feel about the box, what it looks like etc.

Ask the children to turn to the person next to them and arrange themselves in pairs as an A or a B. Show the children the sentence starters:

> Pandora, you should open the box because ...
> Pandora, you should not open the box because ...

Now, in each pair, child A should tell child B why Pandora *should* open the box, then the child B should tell their partner why Pandora *should not* open the box.

Conscience alley

This is a good point to arrange the children into a conscience alley. (The next stages of the lesson described here took place in the hall, where there was plenty of space, but the children could easily be organized in the classroom.)

```
              P

A                         B
A                         B
A             |           B
A             |           B
A             ▼           B
A                         B
```

All the A children should be on one side of the alley and all the B children on the other. Begin with the teacher as Pandora walking down the conscience alley and the children whispering their reasons why he or she as Pandora should or should not open the box. The A children persuade Pandora to open the box and the B children persuade her not to. This can then get louder and louder until the children are nearly shouting.

Then, choose one of the children to take the part of Pandora and walk down the conscience alley. The other children try to persuade her, and this time they have the opportunity to persuade Pandora in their own language. (All the children in the class involved in this session were Punjabi and Urdu speakers.) We observed that some children became more animated when speaking in their home language, others preferred to speak in English – they had the right to choose.

At the end of the conscience alley, the child who is being Pandora is asked which decision she is going to make. In this session, she decided to open the box. If she had not taken this decision, we could have discussed why, and then what might happen if she *did* open the box.

The children were then asked to think about what actually came out of the box – misery, hate, anger – and that these feelings did not exist before the box was opened.

Hot seat

The next step was to set up a hot seat activity. As most of the girls were quite shy, three of them together were asked to be Pandora. The other children had two minutes to discuss with their partner the questions that they would like to ask Pandora. This turned out to be very successful as, by this stage, the children were familiar with the dilemma which was the main focus of the story, and they asked Pandora some very interesting questions.

We then returned to the classroom and the children were asked to make notes on what they had done, ready for the writing session. Soon afterwards, they wrote in the first person about Pandora making the decision to open the box and then how she felt when she realized what had come out of the box. The quality of the writing was very good, because the children had spent so much time discussing the story in a purposeful way.

TALK TO WRITING – SOME SUGGESTIONS FOR TOPICS

Here are some ideas for writing topics for KS2 pupils, which arise from collaborative talk in the classroom. Learning objectives from the National Literacy Strategy are given for each one.

1. Report writing in the style of newsletter, newspaper or magazine:, e.g.
   A heated discussion took place yesterday in the Parish Council meeting, which was called to discuss the proposed development of the playing fields for new low cost housing.

   Year 6, Term 1, text 15 *to develop a journalistic style through considering balanced and ethical reporting, what is of public interest in events*

2. A speech to read out in assembly to give your views on the new arrangements for lunches in school.

   Year 6, Term 2, text 18 *to construct effective arguments, develop a point logically and effectively, support and illustrate points persuasively*
   Year 5, Term 3, text 19 *to construct an argument to persuade others of a point of view, present the case to class or group*
   Year 4, Term 3, text 23 *to present a point of view in writing, linking points persuasively*

3. Write a discussion piece, give the arguments for and against an idea: e.g.
   Should schools stay open until 7pm to provide childcare?

   Year 6, Term 2, text 18 *to construct effective arguments, develop a point logically and effectively, support and illustrate points persuasively*
   Year 5, Term 3, text 19 *to construct an argument to persuade others of a point of view, present the case to class or group*
   Year 4, Term 3, text 23 *to present a point of view in writing, linking points persuasively*

4. Write instructions: e.g. for a friend to tell them how to get to your house from school.

   Year 3, Term 2, text 16 *write instructions, using a range of organizational devices*

5. Compare and contrast poem/story/writer A with writer B.

    Year 4, Term 1, text 7 *to compare and contrast poems on similar themes discussing personal responses and preferences*
    Year 5, Term 1, text 7 *to analyse and compare poetic style, explain and justify personal beliefs*
    Year 6, Term 1, text 5 *to contribute effectively to shared discussion about literature, responding to and building on the views of others*
    Year 6, Term 3, text 5 and 6 *to compare and contrast the work of a single writer, to look at connections and contrasts in the work of different writers*
    Year 6, Term 3 text 12 *to compare texts in writing*

6. A persuasive leaflet: e.g. *Why St Andrew's School is the best in Keighley*

    Year 5, Term 3, text 19 *to present an argument to persuade others of a point of view*

7. History: a speech on Ancient Greece: e.g.
    Why women and slaves should/not be allowed to vote.
    My father, Leonidas, was an excellent leader of the Spartans at Thermopylae even though all the army died.
    What have the Greeks done for us?

    QCA Unit: Ancient Greeks
    Year 6, Term 2, text 18 *to construct effective arguments, develop a point logically and effectively, support and illustrate points persuasively*
    Year 5, Term 3, text 19 *to construct an argument to persuade others of a point of view, present the case to class or group*
    Year 4, Term 3, text 23 *to present a point of view in writing, linking points persuasively*

8. Geography: *Should the new road be built through the village?*

    QCA Unit: Local Studies
    Year 6, Term 2, text 18 *to construct effective arguments, develop a point logically and effectively, support and illustrate points persuasively*
    Year 5, Term 3, text 19 *to construct an argument to persuade others of a point of view, present the case to class or group*
    Year 4, Term 3, text 23 *to present a point of view in writing, linking points persuasively*

CONCLUSION

To sum up this chapter, the box presents some principles for promoting collaborative talk for learning and writing with bilingual pupils.

Summary: Principles for developing talk for learning and writing

- Bilingual pupils need opportunities to learn to talk in English and also to talk in order to learn.
- A classroom that is full of rich, collaborative dialogue provides the best environment for bilingual pupils to learn.
- It is essential to develop a positive classroom ethos to support collaborative talk.
- Collaborative talk always needs to be underpinned by a strong and clear structure.
- The best writing comes from rich, well-supported collaborative talk.

FURTHER READING

Grugeon, Elizabeth, Hubbard, Lorraine, Smith, Carol and Dawes, Lyn (2001) *Teaching Speaking and Listening in the Primary School.* London: David Fulton.

Hodson, Pam and Jones, Deborah (2001) *Teaching Children to Write: The Process Approach.* London: David Fulton.

Chapter 5

Using a 'Bilingual Approach' to Promote Learning: Ideas for Talking and Writing

Jean Conteh and Shila Begum

In this chapter, we explain the importance of allowing bilingual pupils to use all the languages in their repertoires to promote their learning in mainstream classrooms. Then, we suggest ways in which you can do this. We call this a 'bilingual approach' to learning, though in some cases, of course, it may be better described as a 'multilingual approach', as many pupils speak and/or write more than two languages.

WHAT IS A 'BILINGUAL APPROACH' TO LEARNING?

A bilingual approach is *not* about explicitly teaching pupils to speak and write other languages besides English. Rather, it is about opening out to them routes to learning English (and to learning generally) which are not open to them if the whole discourse of the classroom is in English. In this way, pupils gain power over their own learning. There are also ways in which pupils who *don't* speak the languages spoken by their classmates can be included in such an approach, benefiting from increased language awareness and in other ways, as we explained in Chapter 1.

It is important to understand that such an approach can be used by *all* teachers in their own classrooms, not just those who are themselves bilingual. As the activities are described, we provide advice and suggestions on how to do this, including how you can use effectively any bilingual support, for example bilingual assistants, parents, siblings and others who may be available to work with you in your classroom.

It is vital to remember, as we emphasized in Chapter 1, that a bilingual approach is valuable for *all* pupils in your classroom, including those who may not themselves be categorized as bilingual, for the following reasons:

- All pupils need to have the ability to analyse and compare languages – this will increase their language awareness and knowledge about language, and their cognitive capacity generally.

● Talking and thinking about different languages will improve communication between pupils of different language and cultural backgrounds in your class.

● Promoting a positive ethos, which nurtures language diversity, contributes to overcoming conflict in the school and even in the wider community.

When you begin to explore, you may be surprised at the amount of knowledge about different languages that your 'monolingual' pupils already possess. Through using some of the activities described in this chapter, you will be able to draw out this knowledge and engage both bilingual and monolingual pupils alike.

'BEING YOURSELF' AND DEVELOPING CONFIDENCE AS A LEARNER

'If I did not burst out crying it was probably because of anger. I don't know quite why, but I felt angry at myself and at her. I felt I lacked something that everyone else had. I wanted to be someone else. ... How could I tell her that I knew everything she thought I did not know?'

These are the words of a student in her twenties, on a BEd course, who was asked to write about a personal experience that had a profound effect on her decision to train as a primary teacher. She wrote about being a 5-year old, just starting school, and the anger and anxiety she felt when her attempts at explaining something in Punjabi were rebuffed. Her powerful statement about wanting to be 'someone else' illustrates the great dangers in ignoring the knowledge and experience that children bring with them to school, and also shows the links between identity and learning which we discussed in Chapter 1. The languages we speak are part of our identities, and so need to be recognized as part of the way we learn. But this does *not* mean that pupils must be actively taught to speak and write other languages besides English in school – there is not time for this, and it is not part of the mainstream school's responsibility.

The main benefit of a bilingual approach is that it helps pupils to develop confidence in themselves and in their capacities as learners. Pauline Gibbons (1991), working in Australia, suggests there are three significant advantages for pupils' learning if they are allowed to use their full language repertoires in school. In brief, these are:

● It makes it easier for pupils to develop understanding of basic concepts by allowing them to draw on their total language experience.

● It helps develop pupils' confidence and self-esteem.

● It takes advantage of one of the greatest resources children bring to school, and is based on sound pedagogic principles.

These three points focus on different and equally important aspects of learning: cognitive, affective and social. Bilingual pupils need space to find their own ways of using all the languages they know as a tool for their learning. For the teacher, in many ways, this means a change from thinking about what you are going to teach to thinking instead about how your pupils are going to learn. Usually, the main preoccupation of planning is to work out how and what to teach. But, to develop a bilingual approach, you need to think more carefully and analytically about how your pupils are learning.

This need for a switch in focus from teaching to learning can actually feel quite threatening, especially if your pupils speak languages that you, as their teacher, do not understand. It can feel like a shift in power relationships in the classroom. But, if we do not allow pupils to take power over their own learning, we are not helping them to become the confident, independent learners that they need to be in order to succeed. If, however, we think about this shift in power relationships as empowerment, then we are recognizing that giving pupils more control over their own learning does not necessarily mean taking power away from teachers – the experience can be empowering and liberating for all involved.

DEVELOPING A 'BILINGUAL APPROACH' IN THE CLASSROOM

As we suggest in Chapter 7, all schools need a whole-school ethos which values diversity and respects the individuality of all its pupils. In this section we suggest ways in which this ethos of diversity and respect can be promoted within the classroom through developing a bilingual approach. But, this must not be an 'add-on' to the main curriculum and activities of the school. Such an ethos needs to permeate the whole life of the school. Within this atmosphere, a bilingual approach can thrive in the classroom.

To develop a bilingual approach in the classroom, there are two levels and stages of action. The first is to create the kind of classroom ethos where mutual trust and respect are nurtured and pupils, teachers and other adults alike feel it is safe to take risks. The second stage is to adopt a few practical strategies which make space for children to use their different languages in positive ways in their learning. Obviously, these two ways of working go along together; if you begin with promoting a positive ethos, you will find that the space for children to use their different languages will soon open up.

Stage 1: A classroom ethos for promoting language diversity

When you first suggest to pupils that they can speak their home languages in the classroom, it can seem initially a strange and new idea to them. At first, they may feel very self-conscious about using languages publicly which they normally only use privately at home with certain members of their families. They may not understand why you are asking them to do this. This is why the first stage in the process – that of developing a positive classroom ethos – is crucially important. The way you do it needs to key into the specific context of your own classroom, guided by the principles explained here.

You will find it is very helpful to share with your pupils what you are trying to do and why. You could promote a class discussion about the languages they speak and the value of using different languages in the classroom. You may be surprised by the sophistication of your pupils' responses.

These practical suggestions will help you as a teacher to develop a classroom ethos that promotes trust and where all pupils feel secure:

1. Show genuine interest in your pupils' home languages – ask them questions about their languages and whether they are attending different classes or schools outside of mainstream school. They will appreciate your interest and such questions can be excellent sources of information.

2. Turn normal classroom routines into opportunities for multilingual interaction, for example greetings can be done in different languages, the register can be done, as can Maths routines and so on. Your pupils can supply the language information to make the activities happen.

3. Make language diversity part of the visual environment of your classroom. Try to reflect all the languages that the children speak in displays, resources and signs – some of these may be items that your pupils bring in from home.

4. Make language diversity part of the aural environment of your classroom as well as the visual, so that all pupils, including those who are 'monolingual', regularly hear different languages spoken and see different languages written.

5. Make the classroom displays a feature of discussion and classroom learning, and try to change them regularly. *Do not let your displays and other resources fade and gather dust!*

6. Demonstrate to your pupils that bilingual support staff are valued and respected members of the class community and of the school – encourage them to take active roles with all the children in the class, not just the ones perceived as needing extra language support. For example, you could read or tell a dual language story collaboratively for the whole class, with you reading in English and the assistant in his or her language.

Stage 2: Practical strategies to promote a bilingual approach in the classroom

As soon as activities like those in Stage 1 are becoming established routines in your classroom, you can begin to introduce simple practical strategies that help to make the use of different languages part of the ways you work with your pupils in the classroom. Here are a few examples:

1. For activities involving small-group discussion, pupils can be physically grouped in ways that allow them to use their first languages together. Give enough time and privacy in these groups for children to talk to one another, and then ask for a report or some other feedback in English.

2. Build opportunities for children to talk to one another about what they are doing in their stronger languages into as many activities as possible, for example, allow pairs or small groups of same-language speakers to work together on practical or problem-solving tasks.

3. In whole-class discussions, invite bilingual pupils to contribute words and phrases which translate the main ideas being negotiated. This will develop their confidence, making them feel like experts. It will also provide support for pupils who may be struggling with comprehension. This could be developed into a small display showing the alternative words in the different languages.

4. In the Literacy Hour and other sessions with a language focus, invite pupils to think about different languages and how they work; for example, they can compare the ways meanings are expressed and words and sentences are constructed in different languages by looking at poems and other literary texts in different languages.

As time goes on, you will begin to think of ideas like these of your own which fit your own contexts.

BUILDING A BILINGUAL APPROACH INTO CLASSROOM ACTIVITIES

The curriculum primary teachers are expected to teach is so full that it seems to allow no space for individual variation or anything extra. So, rather than thinking of the bilingual approach as something added on, it is more useful to think of ways of building it into ongoing classroom activities and approaches so that it becomes a normal and accepted way of working with your pupils. In this section, we provide some examples of how this can be done, in two main ways:

- Promoting a bilingual approach through creativity.
- Developing activities that allow pupils to take the lead.

Then we end with a section with two parts, which give advice on ways of promoting bilingual learning and also enhancing language and cultural awareness for pupils who may not share the languages spoken by their classmates:

- Working with bilingual support staff and other adults:
  - o developing and using multilingual resources
  - o promoting cultural belonging through language.

PROMOTING A BILINGUAL APPROACH THROUGH CREATIVIY

There is currently much interest in opening out ways and possibilities for pupils to learn across the curriculum through creativity. This can also work very well for promoting the use of different languages in the classroom. Role play and story-based activities allow pupils to use their imaginations and, through this, the opportunities for talk are expanded in a wide range of ways.

For example, a class of reception children, working with Shila Begum, set off on an imaginary journey on a bus, which continued over three weeks. A large, two-dimensional cardboard cutout bus, painted in colours which were familiar to them from local buses, drew the children straight in to the imagined world, helped to make the activity feel real and contextualized it for them. The journey theme gave a strong sense of continuity and progression to the activities, which were designed to give as many opportunities for talk as possible.

Shila and her pupils' 'journey' began with everyone travelling to Bangladesh, then they visited famous sights in the country and a disaster befell them, which was resolved happily. Here is her description of the activities:

Activity: Journeys on the magic bus

Activity 1: The amazing flying bus

I began this activity by discussing the idea of journeys and different types of transport. I told the children that we would be using the bus to travel to Bangladesh. I was not surprised when they told me that this was impossible because we needed a plane to go to Bangladesh. I said it was a magic bus and it could take them anywhere in the world. They quickly accepted the idea of a magic flying bus and got into role immediately. While in the bus, we had lunch, which was rice and curry, and they pretended to eat with their hands. A few pretended to be scared and thought they would fall into the oceans that we were flying over. Some decided to stick their hands out of the window and touch the clouds. We even slept in the bus. The session ended just as we landed in Bangladesh.

Activity 2: Famous sights and the wobbly bridge

I used visual aids to help contextualize this activity, for example pictures of famous buildings and landmarks in Bangladesh. The children pretended to take photographs of the beautiful scenery and talked about what they could see. Our day ended with the children attempting to cross a bridge. However, all of a sudden the bridge started to wobble – what was going to happen next? I decided to end the second session with this cliffhanger.

Activity 3: Let's go fishing

I continued this activity from exactly where we had stopped the previous week; the bridge was still wobbling and we were about to fall! Unfortunately, the bridge gave way and everyone plunged into the sea. Luckily we found a boat and quickly climbed into it. Once in the boat, the children felt hungry and decided to catch some fish for their lunch. While everybody was fishing the children took part in singing the old nursery rhyme 'One two three four five, once I caught a fish alive'. They began by singing this in English and then I surprised them all by asking them to sing the song in Bangla (not all the children were Bangla speakers). To begin with, I sang the song alone while the children listened attentively and soon all the children joined in enthusiastically, including the non-Bangla speakers. I ended the session by giving the children the opportunity to tell me about their adventures from all three sessions.

As the activities progressed over the three sessions, the children used their full language repertoires with growing confidence. This was, no doubt, partly a result of the modelling Shila was able to provide using her own bilingual skills, but it was also promoted by the gradually growing richness of the story context in which all the activities were situated, and the children's developing awareness of this. The story context also served as a means of opening out the children's imaginative responses, as can be seen from the child who, spontaneously and unselfconsciously, suddenly called out in Bangla to his teacher to come and look at the fish he had caught. It is interesting that, though not all the children were Bangla speakers, they joined in the singing of the song spontaneously and enthusiastically.

The following general points are key principles which underpin the success of the activities described above. They can be used as guidelines for planning similar activities around a theme of your own choosing, which you can tailor to suit your own language skills and knowledge and those of bilingual assistants and others who can be involved, the learning needs of your own pupils and the specific learning objectives required by the stage they have reached in the curriculum:

- Activities should build, as far as possible, on pupils' previous experiences and their experiences beyond school.
- As a teacher, you need to show your personal interest and engagement in the activities, for example by taking part along with your pupils, paying attention to consistency in small details, using appropriate body language, facial expressions and so on to help build up the power of the imagined context – this assists your pupils' journey into fantasy and helps to sustain it.
- Pupils' curiosity can be captured at the start of the activity with an interesting artefact, poem, story or picture, and then sustained and extended by the story line as the activities continue – 'cliff hangers', problems, puzzles etc. all work very effectively to do this.
- As the activities progress, build in opportunities for pupils to reflect on what they have done in previous sessions, and how it links with what they are doing currently.
- Encourage talk at all stages by using open-ended questions that promote discussion.
- At times, allow pupils simply to repeat what they hear. This can help to reinforce comprehension and also support pupils who may be new to English.

DEVELOPING ACTIVITIES THAT ALLOW PUPILS TO TAKE THE LEAD

Another type of activity which can encourage pupils to use their full language (and cultural) repertoires confidently to promote learning is those that tap into the knowledge and expertise from family and community experiences. This is sometimes known as the 'funds of knowledge' approach (Moll et al., 1992). This works very well if you can develop broad themes in your planning and, within these, allow pupils to interpret topics in ways that reveal their knowledge of family and community topics and events. Cooking, dress, family celebrations and similar themes are all very valuable in this respect. Pupils can disclose fascinating information that will enrich your lessons as well as your own understanding of their cultural backgrounds.

The 'family trees' activity, which has already been discussed in Chapter 2, is one that would fit well into many different cross-curricular themes, and can develop in many different directions. It is, essentially, very simple, and can be done at different levels with pupils of different ages.

Begin with a discussion with the children about their family members and the different names they have for them. You will find that there may be names for relatives which the children know in their first languages which cannot be directly translated into English because the distinctions that they signal are not made. For example, there are separate words in Punjabi for paternal grand-parents (*dhaadee* and *dhaadah*) and maternal grandparents (*naani* and *naana*), and many other relatives, whereas in English these relationships are not usually differentiated.

Discuss with the children why there may be different words in different languages for family relatives, and compare different ways of naming relatives in different languages. The children may notice some interesting features, for example that the names for 'mother' (*mum*, *amma*, *mama*, *mata*) and 'father' (*daddy*, *abba*, *papa*, *pita*) are similar, and they may have ideas as to why this may be.

After the oral discussion, children can be shown some examples of family trees and they can compare the different ways in which they present the information. Then they can be asked to draw their own, using a framework they are given, or ones they devise themselves.

WORKING WITH BILINGUAL SUPPORT STAFF AND OTHER ADULTS

In the final section of this chapter, we give some ideas for the ways in which different languages can be used in class, first of all as a resource for promoting language and cultural awareness among all pupils, and then as a means of 'unlocking' knowledge for pupils in ways that access to English only may not be able to do.

Developing and using multilingual resources for language awareness

Resources in different languages can promote a bilingual approach to learning through developing pupils' language learning and also their language awareness and knowledge about language. There are many published materials, and home-grown resources can also be produced using the languages that pupils and staff in the school speak. These can be used to promote listening, speaking, reading and writing in primary classrooms. Also, reach out to members of the local community who may be able to help pupils develop understanding through their home languages. Here are a few examples of specific activities.

Multilingual nameplates

To begin developing multilingual resources and to appreciate their potential, a very simple and powerful activity is that of making multilingual nameplates. This also links with the family tree work described earlier, and could be done as a follow-up to this. It can develop into a rich and interesting project in its own right, in which many cross-curricular learning objectives, particularly in

History and RE, can be achieved. Through it, you can find out more about your pupils' knowledge of different languages and scripts and also promote useful discussion about different systems for naming babies, to which the whole class can contribute.

If it is not done as part of a theme or topic, it can be a simple ongoing activity, done when time is available over the course of half a term, with each pupil working to produce their own nameplate.

The activity can develop in the following way:

1. Begin by talking with your pupils about an example of names and naming systems in your own family or community, showing how names can be changed and written in different ways. For example, when I talk about my own name, I describe how it can be changed from 'Jean' to 'Jeanne' or 'Jeanette', and how the boy's name 'John' is really a version of the same name; how, in France, boys can be called 'Jean', which is the French version of 'John', but it is pronounced in a different way.

2. Have versions of your name in different scripts to show your pupils (prepared beforehand by bilingual members of the school). Discuss them, the ways they are written and the differences and similarities between them. If possible, make sure that some of these are in scripts known to some of the pupils in the class, or arrange with a bilingual support assistant to be present to help with the next stage of the activity.

3. Pupils work in groups, each with an 'expert' to produce versions of their names in different spelling and scripts. This needs organizing according to the 'funds of knowledge' available in the class. The experts can be pupils, parents, other family members, support assistants and so on. The aim is for each child to produce a 'nameplate' for their own name on appropriate card or coloured paper, with as many versions of their name as possible. On the back of the plate, they need to provide a key to the versions of their names, explaining the scripts used.

4. As the nameplates are completed, they can be collected in a class book or file, or displayed in the classroom. The activity can be concluded in this way, with an interesting and attractive display, but there are also many possibilities for continuation into Language, History or RE work with investigations into different naming systems, naming practices and so on.

Using dual language books

Besides being useful resources for those pupils who may be new to English but have literacy skills in other languages, dual language books can be used with all pupils to promote language and cultural awareness. Through using and discussing the books, pupils can analyse and compare different languages and scripts. As in the nameplate activity, some pupils in your class may become the 'experts' for specific texts, and you may also need to call on other experts in the school and the community to help gain the full benefit that the texts can provide.

Here are some ideas based on *Send for Sohail!*, which was introduced in Chapter 3, where you will find a page from the book is reproduced (see page 38). The layout of the book offers possibilities for some useful group work, perhaps as a guided reading activity in the Literacy Hour. The children can compare the ways the two texts work (i.e., do they have full stops, capital letters and so on), and look closely at the marks on the page and find repeating words or symbols. If you have an Urdu reader who can oblige (or can read it yourself) a parallel reading of the story can be done – the layout means that both scripts can be followed simultaneously by a small group of children.

Afterwards, individual words can be pointed out, and their repetition in the text tracked, comparing the positions they appear on the page, and the different ways they may be included as part of a sentence or paragraph. Children could be encouraged to make up the next 'adventure' for Sohail, discussing what could happen next, and deciding how to write it.

PROMOTING A SENSE OF CULTURAL BELONGING THROUGH LANGUAGE

Words do not just have dictionary definitions, they also often have strong cultural connotations and echoes which can be fascinating, but can also make them complex to translate and easy to misinterpret. Sometimes, words can have powerful sensory resonances for the speaker or listener, which make them almost untranslatable to someone who does not share the lived experiences they are embedded in. Words can be so powerfully evocative of tastes, smells, sights, sounds and tactile experiences that it is difficult to separate them from these stimuli.

The problem, at times, for the teacher is how to 'unlock' the full, rich meanings of the word for the child. This means, often, bridging the gap between the cultures of home and of school, helping the child to feel that they, and the things they know and have experienced, belong in the classroom and can be part of their new learning. This is doubly difficult when the cultural references may not be shared, or even apparent, in the first place. Here is a small but significant example:

'A 7-year-old child began school in England after spending her early years in Sierra Leone, West Africa. She had a very good experience on the whole, with a sensitive and perceptive teacher who worked hard to help her to make the transition into a new school system. There were a few hitches. One day, in a science activity, the teacher asked her to balance the plastic classroom scales, expecting her to respond quickly and enthusiastically, as usual. But, this time, the response was nothing more than a confused look. In Sierra Leone, to 'balance' something means to carry it on your head. So the confused look was not just incomprehension, but a reflection of the child's struggle to harmonize two very different meanings for one word.'

In this case, in discussion with the child's parent (who in fact was one of the authors), the confusion was cleared up, the science learning was not impaired and – more importantly – the child's enthusiasm for learning continued to grow. This may not have been the case if communication between home and school had not been so positive or the teacher had not had the professional space to use her judgement to decide what to do to help her new pupil over this and similar semantic hurdles. Underpinning this, the teacher had the strong belief that, through accessing the knowledge which the child brought to the classroom, she would not only help her to feel that she belonged, but would more easily find ways to help her develop confidence in the new knowledge and cultural practices she was entering into.

When such cultural bridging involves the use of different languages, the role of the bilingual assistant (or teacher, if available) becomes vital. By the use of a few well-chosen words in first language, comprehension can be achieved and – even more important – pupils can be helped to feel that they, and who they are, belong in the classroom. Here is another brief example from personal observation:

'The teacher, Shaheen, was working with her Year 5 class (about half of them Punjabi speakers) on the topic of Egyptians and was using drama to help them understand the cycle of farming, dependent on the seasonal flooding of the land by the river Nile. The children were role playing farmers, turning over the muddy, silt-enriched soil with their hoes. Shaheen spoke in English, describing how the land was tilled and prepared for the seed to be planted. At one point, briefly, she switched to Punjabi. When the lesson finished, I [Jean Conteh] asked her what she had said in Punjabi. She explained that she had described to the children how she had seen water running through irrigation channels on a recent visit to Pakistan and this had made her think about how the soil and mud must have felt on the ancient Egyptian farmers' feet as they worked in the fields flooded by the river.'

The codeswitching was very brief, entirely natural and within the flow of the talk in the lesson. None of the children who did not speak Punjabi seemed to pay much attention to it. Shaheen said that she did this kind of thing as often as she could, but always briefly, making sure that any information conveyed in Punjabi was also covered in English. She believed strongly that her use of codeswitching allowed an extra 'way in', enriching the learning for those children who could access it. We would suggest, also, that it offered a valuable lesson in language awareness to the monolingual children in the class.

For the 'monolingual' teacher to provide this kind of learning opportunity, it is, of course, essential to involve bilingual assistants and other adults in the planning and preparation of the teaching as much as possible. They may be able to point out aspects of the language that may cause difficulty, and to advise on ways to key into children's home and community experiences in positive and productive ways. So, they can become a resource to support and develop learning potential for all the bilingual pupils, not just for those who may be deemed in need of 'support'.

If they cannot be present at the time the activity is being carried out, it may be possible to have one of the more knowledgeable pupils in the class take on the role of 'bilingual consultant' for the course of the activity. The key to success in this kind of approach is to recognize and value the diversity of expertise of all members of the school and the community to which it belongs.

CONCLUSION

To sum up, some key principles for using a bilingual approach to promote learning in primary classrooms are presented in the box.

Summary: Key principles for developing a 'bilingual approach' to promote learning

- A 'bilingual approach' opens out routes to learning for bilingual pupils, and enhances language and cultural awareness for all pupils.
- For some bilingual pupils, a 'bilingual approach' can be an important contribution to self-confidence and a sense of identity.
- Specific bilingual strategies and approaches need to be introduced within a positive and supportive whole-class ethos.
- Activities that promote the use of imagination and creativity are excellent also for promoting a bilingual approach to learning.
- In many activities, bilingual pupils can take the lead, bringing knowledge from home and community contexts to inform the learning.
- Bilingual staff in the school need to play a vital and flexible role in planning and implementing a bilingual approach, and their contribution needs to be facilitated.

FURTHER READING

Gibbons, Pauline, (1991) *Learning to Learn in a Second Language*. Sydney, NSW: Primary English Teaching Association.

Gregory, Eve, Long, Susie and Volk, Dinah (eds) (2004) *Many Pathways to Literacy: Young Children Learning with Siblings, Grandparents, Peers and Communities*. London: RoutledgeFarmer.

Moll, Luis et al. (1992) Funds of Knowledge for Teaching: Using a Qualitative Approach to Connect Homes and Classrooms, *Theory into Practice*, 31 (2), pp. 132–141.

NOTE

Send for Sohail! was produced by teachers and students from the Department of Teacher Education at Bradford College. Copies can be ordered via the departmental website: www.bilk.ac.uk/college/depts/teached/.

Chapter 6

Using Drama to
Promote Learning

Alex Fellowes

THE IMPORTANCE OF DRAMA IN THE CLASSROOM

Drama is both a most effective and a powerful learning medium. It can transform the learning environment for many children, not just bilingual pupils. It works at many conceptual, creative, physical and emotional levels. It is also an immensely flexible tool for the teacher and can be applied right across the curriculum.

It provides the teacher with a great deal of scope for promoting learning within the classroom, in the following ways:

- **It extends children's language.** It provides pupils with an exciting range of opportunities to develop their talk in real-life role play situations. Because talk is such an essential element in the dramatic process, it enables children to do this in the most natural and active ways. It also gives the teacher, in role, the chance to model language through the activities themselves and introduce language forms into the activity that the children would not normally encounter.

- **It allows children to work at many different language levels.** In drama activities pupils are enabled to use talk for a range of different purposes and for a range of different audiences. Again, this is an integral part of drama as a creative activity. Within drama situations children will find themselves using language to persuade, inform, report, argue and so on, and will be asked to adapt their talk for a situation-specific purpose and for the audience intended.

- **It promotes learning and cognitive development.** As Chapter 4 demonstrates, talk lies at the heart of the whole learning process. Through talk, children are developing their thinking skills and drama gives them the means to talk and therefore think at so many different levels, in the most stimulating and active way.

- **It develops higher order thinking skills.** Built into drama activities are opportunities for children to project, resolve dilemmas, provide information, hypothesize, give explanations and solve problems. All these things are at the core of drama as an experience.

- **It promotes listening as well as talk.** For drama to be a really successful vehicle, children need to develop skills as listeners as well as talkers. All drama activities require a vital listening element, either asking children to follow instructions and directions or respond to one another's role play. Pupils also need to learn what it is to be a 'good audience' as well as an active participant.

- **It provides a powerful stimulus for creative writing and develops literacy.** Children cannot write creatively in a vacuum or by a formula of monotonous tasks. Creativity is driven by imagination. Drama furnishes pupils with the imaginative experiences to inspire their writing. Because it works at an emotional and physical level, children can draw very easily from these memorable experiences and translate them very effectively to their writing. Through drama work, children are also encouraged to read for a range of purposes and, most importantly, for meaning. This also is a natural element in the process. It can be a real motivation for children to extend their reading and to access more challenging texts.

- **It nurtures social skills.** An intrinsic element in every drama activity is communication and cooperation. Children are asked to work in pairs, in groups and as a whole class. Through drama work they learn to respect other children's ideas and feelings, build empathy with one another and develop cooperative attitudes. Indeed these social skills are a fundamental constituent of dramatic activity. Drama is also a learning activity whose success depends upon self-discipline – something not so much imposed from without, but rather developed from within.

After being a teacher for 30 years who always used drama as a vehicle for learning across the curriculum, over the past five years I have redirected my teaching career to taking drama workshops into schools and, through active drama experience, provided access for KS1 and 2 pupils to literature and different areas of the curriculum. This has given me a unique insight into the effectiveness of drama as a learning medium and also a unique opportunity to develop a wide repertoire of drama activities and conventions. I have also been invited to lead staff development focusing upon drama as a learning vehicle across the curriculum and, more specifically, on how it can be employed to promote talking and listening and, related to these, literacy.

In my travels I have found that many teachers would be very willing to use drama as a teaching tool, but feel that they don't have sufficient 'know-how' to do so and also are a little anxious about the risks that might be involved in this kind of active learning medium. I therefore wish to set out the approach I employ and demonstrate the methods I find successful through a practical example of my work.

From my own personal experience the key element of a successful drama lesson is:

structure

Structure reduces risks to a minimum and gives the teacher the means to control the activity. It is also important to provide children with the support – the 'scaffolding' – that they need to develop their drama skills and build their confidence in responding to a range of challenging learning situations. Writing frames are an invaluable support for enabling children to become more competent and skilled writers; structure has the same objective in drama work. It establishes a framework within which children have:

- Clear starting out points
- A definite direction to their talk and role play
- A real sense of purpose in their activities.

By establishing structure in their drama work, teachers provide their pupils with a springboard to express themselves more and more creatively and consequently to extend their language use and their thinking skills.

The rest of this chapter consists of a case study describing an example of a successful drama project I have done. This will give a framework for teachers to follow in developing drama projects in their own classrooms.

AN EXAMPLE OF SUCCESSFUL DRAMA PRACTICE

Frankenstein in Year 5

I love to introduce primary pupils to great stories from literature through drama. In this way, a perfect opportunity is provided to expose them to some of its text. Because the text is delivered in short, manageable extracts and is embedded within a drama activity, the children will make sense of its language in the context of their role play. It is extremely empowering for children to use the language of Shakespeare, Dickens, the Brontes, Mary Shelley and so on in such an active and dynamic way. In this way drama can raise the 'language stakes' of the learning environment.

Another reason for using such a challenging story as Mary Shelley's *Frankenstein* is that it appeals especially to the imagination of boys (although girls love it too – it was a woman who wrote it!). Some boys find it hard to 'engage' in the classroom. The daily routine of the Literacy Hour can fail to motivate and inspire them. They need a chance to engage at a more emotional and physical level with the learning. They need a more powerful stimulus and opportunities to learn in different ways.

This case study describes a progression of drama activities related to *Frankenstein*. My own comments on the activities are included.

Hot seating and teacher in role

I began by going into role as Captain Robert Walton, the commander of the ship at the beginning of the novel who is attempting to discover a North West Passage through the Arctic Sea. For this I prepared a monologue.

If hot seating is going to be a successful activity, children need to have something to inspire their questions and responses. I always do my best to 'find the voice' of any character I am going into the hot seat as and speak with their voice. This gives the children something real to work with. The more you as the teacher put into the drama activity in the way of structure, the more you will get out of the pupils in response.

▶

Before actually taking the hot seat, I also tell the group clearly when I will be going into role. For this it is essential to provide oneself with some 'role signifier' such as a hat or a piece of clothing or perhaps even a significant prop. Then you say:

'When I wear this coat I will become [the character].
When I take it off I will return to being myself.'

Children need these clear lines of demarcation in drama work, especially when as a teacher one is assuming a role.

As Captain Walton I explained the reason for this perilous journey (seeking fame and fortune, discovering new sea routes and lands) and the challenges my crew and I have encountered. The pupils were then asked to go into pairs and on a slip of paper devise a question to ask the Captain about what he just said.

I think it is very important here for children to be given some 'thinking time' rather than launching straight into the hot seating. They need time to formulate appropriate questions to gain the information they need for a particular purpose – in this case, working out some of Captain Walton's character traits. So often, it is the teacher who asks the children all the questions. Children don't have too many opportunities to formulate questions themselves, yet this capacity is crucial to the whole learning process.

The teacher 'going into role' is a vital element to the success of drama work in the classroom. By doing this, you can provide a catalyst to the role play and talk of the children and can influence it from within in a non-didactic way. You also have the opportunity to challenge the children's responses, provide vital information and knowledge, raise issues, inject new language and vocabulary and move the drama on if required. This extremely effective drama convention also enables the teacher to share the whole learning experience with the children themselves. This makes for a wonderfully productive relationship between learner and teacher.

Role cards, mime and building belief

The children were then asked to assume the roles of Captain Walton's crew struggling to free the huge sailing ship from its shackles of ice. They were given role cards stating clearly what 'task' they had to perform, for example:

- 'hacking ice off the side of the ship with picks';
- 'mending some of the broken sail';
- 'making fires for cooking and warming themselves' ... and so on.

I made it very clear how I wanted this activity to develop:

1. You must all spread out and sit in your own space.
2. Next, you must make a statue of yourselves doing what it says on the card.
3. When the music starts, you must then bring your character to life ... but in slow motion.

I modelled what this might look like with one of the tasks.

> Using this very structured sequence of activities gives the children a sense of purpose and security. Providing an emotive piece of music (I like music from film scores because they are composed to create a dramatic effect on an audience) can really 'lift' an activity like this and invest it with a strong sense of atmosphere. Very physical drama like this also encourages the pupils to commit themselves to the pretence of the drama and build belief in it.
>
> I often use the convention of 'slow motion' movement in this kind of physical theatre. It helps the children to put detail into their mime and it provides a much-needed control element in an action sequence. Children have a natural inclination to work at a 'Formula 1' pace. They need a dramatic device that will slow them down.

Having got the pupils to set the scene and establish physically the dramatic context, I then told them I'd be going back into role as Captain Walton as they were performing their tasks again. Following the same sequence of activities as before, I proceeded to go round the ship cajoling the crew to redouble their efforts in an unreasonable manner!

Prompt cards for debate and negotiation

The pupils were then told that they were on the verge of mutiny. They have decided to 'down tools' and demand an immediate meeting with the captain.

To facilitate this scene, I prepared beforehand a number of statements that could be 'planted' with crew members (they have to be good readers). These included the following examples:

- 'Captain, we can't go on like this. If the cold doesn't kill us, the polar bears will!'
- 'Captain, this is now useless! There's no way we can carry on this journey. We are stuck fast in the ice. We must turn back!'
- 'Captain, maybe you don't have a family, but we do and we want to be alive to see them again.'

Once more I went into role as Captain Walton and as each of the 'plants' in the crew pronounced their statements, I answered back in a confrontational manner. This helped to heighten the dramatic tension and triggered a really lively debate in which the children got more heated and committed about their arguments in opposition to mine.

> The teacher taking an opposition role is very motivating for the children and also provides an opportunity for challenging the pupils' thinking and extending the debate into new areas. The prompt cards have the same function as script, but with a vital difference: they provide a 'trigger' and a starting-point for creative discussion generated by a very specific dramatic situation. This type of scaffolding has a crucial function in developing dramatic action and language.

Having had this debate with the Captain, the pupils then went off into groups to decide upon three demands to put to him. The framework had now been created for a meeting in which spokespersons from each group presented their legitimate demands to me in role and I attempted to fob them off. This made for yet more lively and vociferous discussion. The more unreasonable I got, the more 'verbal' the children became. The tension and conflict inherent in this dramatic situation was the fuel for the role play and the discussion. Talk arose out of a genuine need to communicate. Also this was a wonderful platform for developing negotiation skills.

Chain of rumours, tableaux and thought tracking

Next, an extract from the actual text of Mary Shelley's novel was used as a stimulus for a drama game. The text selected was this:

We were nearly surrounded by ice, which closed in the ship on all sides, scarcely leaving her the sea-room in which she floated ... About two o'clock the mist cleared away, and we beheld, stretched out in every direction, vast plains of ice, which seemed to have no end ... when a strange sight suddenly attracted our attention ... We saw a low carriage, fixed on a sledge and drawn by dogs, pass on towards the north ... a being which had the shape of a man, but of gigantic stature ... We watched the rapid progress of the traveller with our telescopes until he was lost in the vast wastes of ice ...

The pupils were organized into groups of 10. They were then asked to make tableaux showing the sailors huddled together nervously, some looking with telescopes at the gigantic figure in the distance. With them 'locked' into the tableaux, I next played the sound of a terrible howl (taken from the most recent *Frankenstein* film) and asked them to move into the next frame showing their terrified responses with facial and physical gestures. Afterwards everybody in each tableau had to remember their 'thoughts' at that exact moment in time and the group had to pronounce these in sequence.

This dramatic convention is called thought tracking (rather like having 'thought bubbles'). It is a very effective device and promotes a real sense of focus to the drama work.

As a direct spin-off from all of this, I had some pre-prepared 'rumours' based upon the sighting of the huge being in the sledge. These included:

- I couldn't believe the size of that 'thing' out there. It was at least 8 foot tall!
- Did you see the speed his sledge was travelling? It must have been about 50 mph!
- That gigantic person wasn't human! And I wouldn't like to be around if he comes here.

Selected pupils were given these rumours. On an agreed signal they had to find someone else and tell them what it was. Everyone then had to pass on to someone else the 'rumour' they had just heard (a bit like Chinese Whispers) until the rumours had been circulated right round the class.

Children find games like this a lot of fun and they are very motivated by them. This particular one is excellent for promoting listening skills. It is also a far more interesting way of disseminating information. I don't like doing drama games just for the sake of it (for example, as warm-ups). I think they should be adapted as an integral element of a specific drama activity.

Text as a drama stimulus: introducing a bilingual element

Building on the previous game, I then led the drama into the next phase, introducing Victor Frankenstein into the story.

As before, we used Mary Shelley's book as a stimulus, working on this passage:

I went upon the deck and found all the sailors busy on one side of the vessel, apparently talking to someone in the sea. It was in fact a sledge which had drifted towards us in the night on a large fragment of ice. Only one dog remained alive; but there was a human being within it ... The sailors were persuading him to enter the vessel. He was not as the other traveller seemed to be, a savage inhabitant of some undiscovered land ... When I appeared on deck, the Master said, 'Here is our captain, and he will not allow you to perish in the sea.'

I like to 'break up' a piece of text like this into smaller parts and then share them out to a selection of readers. As these short passages are read out in sequence, everyone else forms a tableau depicting themselves on deck communicating with the mysterious visitor. One pupil in the meantime has been put into role as this person.

In pairs the children were next asked to think of something to say to this desperate man to persuade him to come aboard. The pupils wrote these down on slips of paper and then compared them with others so there was not too much repetition. Once more the tableau was created and, on an agreed signal, the 'sailors' tried to persuade the man in the sledge to come aboard.

Having persuaded him to come aboard, I took advantage of the bilingual skills of most of the pupils to give the drama a new angle and a real boost. Victor Frankenstein was Swiss, so would have spoken a different language to the English-speaking crew. So I asked pupils in role only to answer people's questions in 'first language'. We pretended that there was one person on board who could speak his language and act as a translator. I then gave the pupil in role as Frankenstein a 'fact sheet' about the character with a number of simple bullet points, something like this:

- I come from near Lake Geneva in Switzerland.
- I am a scientist.
- I used to have a family, but there is no one left any more.
- I'm following someone who is very dangerous.
- Everyone must help me to find this person and to destroy him.

It is important that this fact sheet does not give the whole game away.

> Bringing in this bilingual element enhances the whole drama and language experience. It contributes a real sense of dramatic tension, realism and contrast to the role play. It also presents the main participants with a greater range of dramatic options. Where you have pupils with bilingual skills, it seems to me a dreadful waste, especially in drama work, to completely ignore their skills within the learning situation. Sometimes there is a tendency to belittle the language skills that children from a South Asian background bring to school. Perhaps the same attitude would not be so apparent if the children spoke a European language like French, German or Spanish. There is also the mistaken idea that first language use has a detrimental influence on second language development. The research of many prominent educationalists has proved the complete opposite.

Chamber theatre and the 'collective character'

Following Mary Shelley's original novel, the class was asked to listen to Victor Frankenstein's story as told to Robert Walton in his cabin.

I began with a flashback to his childhood and, using a new drama teaching convention, chamber theatre, got the children to find out about his childhood. I prepared a series of complaints received by Frankenstein's father about his son. These included:

- Victor, I've been informed by your sister that she found you in the shed at the end of the garden cutting up small animals ... The neighbours are beginning to talk!
- Victor, the tutor is complaining that you will not do your English and French lessons. That tutor costs me a lot of money, you know ...
- Victor, there are complaints from the servants about your dangerous experiments ... They informed me that there was an explosion in the conservatory, is that true?

Using six prepared statements like this, I asked each of them to be 'owned' by a different pair. The pairs had to work out the most forceful way of delivering these complaints to 'young Frankenstein'. In doing this they assumed the collective role of Frankenstein's father. I assumed a new role, the young Frankenstein, and proceeded to argue back very petulantly to all these criticisms. The children, adopting the collective role as my father, all sat in a very formal way at the end of the room (making it look a little bit like a trial). The rest of the class formed the audience.

Having completed this, I then told the audience in pairs to think of a question or statement to challenge the young Frankenstein about his behaviour and the disrespectful way he talked to his father. This then developed into hot seating.

> Chamber theatre is an immensely useful and flexible device. The main constituent in it is prepared lines delivered by pupils in role, supported by some narrative which provides a catalyst for a piece of improvisation to develop. It establishes the dramatic context for the action and gives

the participants the framework to move the drama forward. I also employed the convention of the 'collective character' which has its roots in the Greek chorus. For children who are quieter and more reserved this gives them the chance to perform with a degree of anonymity.

Forum theatre and the 'active audience'

After the tragic death of Victor Frankenstein's mother, he won a place at the University of Ingolstadt. I then led the children into this new phase of the narrative by asking them to go into role as the young scientist's friends and, in groups of five, think of a really appropriate present to give him at a 'surprise party' organized by his father just before his departure.

An area in the hall was organized as the party room. The 'guests' took their places there in complete silence while I, as Frankenstein, was led there, blindfolded, by a classroom assistant in role as my father. All the children had been told to shout 'hooray' as the blindfolds came off. This made for a really lively and amusing beginning to the activity. I then led the whole group in some 'toasts' to build the party atmosphere and to add some more fun to the festivities.

Introducing rituals like this is another good way of building belief in a dramatic situation as well as giving the pupils a clear framework within which to work and express themselves.

Group by group, the children were then asked to bring me their imaginary presents. With some I showed delight, with others extreme scorn and ingratitude. They had the right to answer me back if they were inclined (and most were!).

The party ended on a very serious note with my father presenting me with a present from my mother for this exact occasion ... a beautifully leather-bound journal containing empty pages, something to which I reacted badly in role.

In pairs, the children were encouraged to work out the exact reason why Frankenstein's mother chose a book with blank pages. On a slip of paper they then had to write a 'message from the grave' from his mother.

The convention employed here, forum theatre, I find flexible, exciting and very productive. Augusto Boal, a Brazilian, pioneered this method. He used it with adults in under-privileged communities to explore vital issues about their lives through drama experience and, through this active process, to enable them to find solutions regarding the problems affecting their lives. Because his methods are so interactive and dynamic, and develop things like problem-solving, negotiation and projection, they are also ideally suited to drama in the classroom. The linchpin to his dramatic practice is the concept of the active audience – participants rather than spectators. Children are encouraged to take on the role of an active audience that can make a direct impact on the development of the dramatic action.

Although in the last sequence I was the principal protagonist alongside the classroom assistant, the development of the drama was shaped and 'directed' by the 'active audience' in role as the party guests. In using the active audience convention with primary children, I prefer to find dramatic situations in which the audience is an integral part of the action itself and has the opportunity to interact with the main characters in a free and dynamic way. The teacher is fulfilling the role as the 'facilitator', but from inside the drama itself.

Montage and framing: a springboard for 'promenade theatre'

We continued to develop Mary Shelley's story through a combination of hot seating, tableaux, forum theatre, rumour chains and thought tracking, focusing upon the young scientist's activities as a student at university with particular attention to his 'laboratory' and his gruesome experiments.

The narrative's attention shifted to the 'creature' he created and unwittingly let loose upon the world. I decided upon working on the creature's first steps into human society and the challenges he was confronted with. To do this I put the children into four different groups and issued each with a task sheet giving instructions for creating a tableau. These tableaux represented hypothetical situations that the creature might encounter on the first part of his journey and were inspired by his account later on of his 'progress' to his creator. These were:

- A family, whose wagon had lost a wheel, stranded in a remote forest with night fast approaching; facing the danger of attacks by wolves or brigands.
- A group of children foolishly playing next to a dangerous wall on the point of collapse.
- A family struggling to pull up turnips from a frozen field.
- A traveller being set upon by cut-throats.

Having done that, each group was then asked to move their tableau forward to the next 'frame'. They were then told to repeat this process one more time, so they would end up with three separate 'frames'. Afterwards, on an agreed signal, the groups in slow motion had to move from one frame to another (montage). They were then encouraged to provide 'thought bubbles' for each of the tableau – bringing words to the freeze frames.

Then I myself went into role as the creature. I made my character really struggle with language, finding it very hard to express myself. I told the class that the drama space would now become the 'journey' that the creature took and that the drama would move round the room – happening where I arrived. As I approached a group, they had to 'act out' their prepared tableau then freeze frame. At that moment the 'creature' would engage with the group and the drama would develop (promenade theatre). Everyone else not involved would be the audience until it was their turn. Because of the creature's immense strength, he was able to offer each group help, but how would they react to this and how would they try to communicate with him?

'Deskilling' oneself in role as the creature in this manner is an extremely effective way of empowering the children within the role play. It has the effect of passing the initiative in the scene to them and giving them the opportunity to shape the drama and decide on outcomes.

Conscience alley

The concluding activity in the workshop involved a drama convention called a 'conscience alley'. This drama structure provides children with an opportunity to be reflective and to explore issues underlying the narrative and the behaviour of any given character in the story. (A conscience alley is also described in use in the Pandora's Box activity described in Chapter 4.)

For Victor Frankenstein to create such a being and then to abandon him completely, deserves some 'come-back'. In pairs, the pupils were therefore asked to prepare a question or a statement that would challenge Frankenstein and his behaviour. Having done this, the children made a 'human passage' through which I, in role as the scientist, had to walk. As I 'ran the gauntlet', the pupils stopped and challenged me. I had to try to justify myself and my actions.

If the teacher wanted to raise any specific issues which the children might not think of themselves, he or she might provide some of the children with 'prompt cards'. This type of scaffolding can raise the whole level of the subsequent exchanges as well as injecting the activity with new language and ideas.

Follow up

Such rich and structured drama work offers a great wealth of activities for promoting talk. After a suitable pause for reflection, it could also lead on to powerful writing. Here are just a few ideas for writing topics based on the Frankenstein project:

- Writing in character: Frankenstein's father or mother.
- The young Frankenstein's sister keeping a diary where she records her brother's strange habits.
- A member of the crew keeping a log of the voyage.
- Poems about the scenery of the voyage, the cold, or the experiences of being a crew member.
- A newspaper article describing the first appearance of the terrible creature invented by Frankenstein.

CONCLUSION

This chapter has focused on the use of drama to promote learning. The box sums up the main points that emerge from the Frankenstein project which serve as a guide for teachers planning their own drama work.

Summary: Principles for successful drama work

- Successful drama activities need a strong and explicit structure.
- 'Good' literature provides powerful stories and also memorable text on which to base drama activities.
- Children need time to absorb what is being asked of them, and develop ideas to contribute to the drama.
- As a teacher, take part in the drama as much as possible – share the learning experiences with your pupils.
- Set up a conflict – a situation where pupils (in role) need to oppose a story or forceful character.
- Build bilingualism into the activity as much possible, providing opportunities for pupils to use their first languages in role.
- Involve as many pupils as possible for short periods through devices like collective character and active audience.

FURTHER READING

Bolton, Gavin (1995) (with Dorothy Heathcote) *Drama for Learning: Dorothy Heathcote's Mantle of the Expert Approach to Education.* Portsmouth, NJ: Heinemann.

Fellowes, Alex (2001) *Bilingual Shakespeare: A Practical Approach for Teachers.* Stoke-on-Trent: Trentham Books.

Neelands, Jonathan (1984) *Making Sense of Drama: A Guide to Classroom Practice.* Oxford: Heinemann Educational Books.

Chapter 7

Promoting a Positive Whole-School Ethos

Ishrat Dad and Angie Kotler

PROVIDING ALL PUPILS WITH OPPORTUNITIES FOR SUCCESS

In this chapter we describe some successful projects and activities that have helped to promote a positive attitude towards diversity in a range of different schools, in order to contribute towards the potential for success for bilingual learners, and – indeed – all learners. Promoting a positive, inclusive classroom and school ethos helps to ensure that all children are able to maximize their full potential. To contribute to this, there are details in this chapter of:

● Ways of meeting the educational needs of bilingual pupils in 'mainly white' settings (written by Ishrat Dad)
● Examples of writing activities that help to develop language and cultural awareness among all pupils (written by Ishrat Dad)
● Projects that link schools with different populations of pupils in order to promote community cohesion and optimize opportunities for learning (written by Angie Kotler).

All pupils, irrespective of their language background, culture, gender, ability, sexuality, social background, or religion are entitled to a good quality education. This education should take place in a safe, supportive environment which enables children to achieve their full potential and also recognizes and caters for their specific needs. It should enable children to understand their rights and responsibilities as citizens in a culturally diverse society. It should prepare them to live in and contribute to a pluralist, inclusive and democratic society in the future.

The National Curriculum, Handbook for Teachers in England (DfEE/QCA, 1999) states:

> Schools have a responsibility to provide a broad balanced curriculum for all pupils. This statutory statement outlines how teachers can modify, as necessary, the National Curriculum programmes of study to provide pupils with relevant and challenging work at each Key Stage.

In the following examples, we show how, through using and modifying elements of the National Curriculum, we can set high expectations of success for our learners, with maximum support and encouragement.

SOME THOUGHTS ABOUT TERMINOLOGY

Sometimes, ethnic minority pupils in 'mainly white' schools are known as 'isolated learners'. This can have a negative connotation, suggesting pupils who are somehow cut off from others in the school. It is also the case that some schools cater for 'ethnic minority' pupils who are actually 'white'. All of these labels are awkward and do not fully reflect the complexity and fluidity of different situations. It is important that all pupils, no matter what their language or cultural background, feel that they belong in their schools. As we showed in Chapters 2 and 3, a sense of belonging is vital for all pupils, not just those starting school for the first time, if they are going to learn to their fullest capacity. Here, Ishrat Dad talks about the role that language can play in promoting a sense of belonging (for both teachers and pupils) in school. This is a practical example of the principles we suggested in Chapter 1:

'As a bilingual teacher from an ethnic minority background, I appreciate and understand some of the obstacles faced by ethnic minority pupils in "mainly white" schools and issues related to their language learning and learning in general. Being able to converse with children from minority backgrounds in their mother tongue has facilitated my teaching. For a monolingual teacher, the same benefits can be gained by being aware of, recognizing and valuing what the child is trying to do with language. Talking with the child, and asking them about their language experiences outside of school will give you an insight into the child's mother tongue, and also ways in to helping them realize their full capabilities.'

SETTLING IN

At first, some minority ethnic children may not be orally confident in school, and this may stem from a number of factors to do with events and issues both inside and outside school. In school, the approach must be to show a positive attitude towards the child, encourage them to play with other children and help them take part in social activities in class. Leaving the child on their own in the hope that they will in time begin to approach others can make it more difficult for them to change their behaviour. In class discussion, the teacher needs to stop to talk to children in turn, and include the bilingual pupil as much as possible. From time to time, during lessons, the teacher can sit down beside the child to work and read together.

Bilingual pupils who are new to the class may need support and encouragement until friendships are created and sustained. Involving the child in becoming an active learner through making comments directly to them about the activity will develop a sense of inclusion. The lack of confidence will gradually decline and the child will become immersed in activities, gain confidence and make relationships with peers more easily. A little tolerance can go a long way. Teachers and adults in school should show understanding and continue to demonstrate care and interest. Reach out to the child regularly and provide numerous opportunities for them to take part in activities, even when these are not taken up on first invitation.

As Chapter 2 showed, having effective links with parents and other carers is an important and integral part of improving the quality of educational provision and raising standards for the new pupil. Families must feel welcome and be reassured that their home values will be recognized and respected. Establishing an effective dialogue between home and school is important as it engages parents in initiatives and can stress the importance of their child's learning. Small details can count for a lot, as in the next example.

'For example, my role as a teacher in a "mainly white" school has helped to affirm a positive sense of identity and belonging in minority ethnic group children in the school. The following is a conversation with a Year 4 pupil, Sajid:

Sajid: Do you have a roza, Miss Dad? (i.e. Are you fasting, Miss Dad?)
Miss Dad: Yes, I have kept ten so far.

Sajid was a quiet child and was not keen to use his mother tongue in front of his peers. However, as we built our relationship teacher to pupil, I found it interesting that Sajid began using Punjabi words to communicate with me. The word "roza" has both religious and cultural connotations. I always try to respond in a way that shows I am aware of such connotations in what children say.'

Finding out about children's languages is vital, as was suggested in Chapter 1. The next page offers a sheet that can be used to find out about the languages children use at home and at school.

Languages I Can Speak/Read/Write

Name: Date:

At Home

When I speak to my mum/dad I speak in (name language, e.g. Punjabi) ....

When I speak to my grandpa/grandma I speak in ....

My older brother/sister speaks to me in ....

My younger brother/sister speaks to me in ....

When I speak to my friend .... (name), I speak in ....

At the synagogue/church/mosque/temple I speak in ....

At home I am learning to read/write/speak:

Read: .... Write: .... Speak: ....

At home I have books written in ....

At home the language I use the most is ....

At School

At playtime I speak in ....

In the classroom I speak in ....

At school, the language I use the most is ....

PROMOTING A POSITIVE, INCLUSIVE CLASSROOM AND SCHOOL ETHOS

Successful implementation of school policies on equality and race relations are central to promoting pupils' learning and attainment. A clear policy that explains the behaviour which will be tolerated goes together with an inclusive curriculum and resources, underpinned by an expectation of equal treatment for all members of the school community.

Racism takes many forms: many ethnic minority pupils face direct racism, and this can start at a very early age. Pupils need support to deal with racist incidents. They need to be taught strategies to report any incidents. Setting up a school council and having 'speak out boxes' where pupils can post any concerns can help.

But racial harassment may not always be explicit: minority ethnic pupils may be teased about their names or appearance. Teachers can stereotype without intending to, which can quickly result in low self-esteem, damaging pupils' sense of self-identity, and making them feel inferior. This can affect their behaviour, motivation and self confidence and result in underachievement.

Equally, it is important that white pupils learn to respect and value others. They must not be led to believe that children from different backgrounds are somehow less human, reinforcing false notions of their superiority. It is important that ethnicity is not seen – for example, through everyday images seen on the television – in an unquestioned negative way as merely to do with poverty, disease or being unfortunate. Pupils need time to discuss the things they see and hear on TV. Asking children to write their responses to international, national or local news can be very illuminating. For example, Jenny's diary writing, shown in Figure 7.3 shows how she constructed her own understanding of the 2004 Indian Ocean tsunami from what she heard on the radio. As well as giving the child a space to try out ideas, opinions and viewpoints, this gives the teacher an opportunity to follow up any issues which may be seen as difficult for individual children, which may involve challenging parents and negative views from the wider culture. Most of these issue-based goals can be brought together and delivered through appropriate PSCHE units or History units.

Creating an inclusive classroom and school should take account of the backgrounds and interests of all pupils. An inclusive classroom needs to take account of teaching styles, management approaches and assessment, so it will enable full participation and raise standards for all pupils. In an inclusive classroom, our expectations of ethnic minority pupils should be high and they should be supported, targeted, monitored and evaluated to raise attainment.

PROMOTING A POSITIVE ETHOS USING WRITING

In the following two sections, we provide suggestions for activities using writing which help promote a positive ethos in schools. The first section is about using writing to promote a sense of belonging in the classroom, and the second is about promoting language and cultural awareness for all pupils through writing.

A sense of belonging: bringing the world into the classroom

Allowing children to have ownership and a genuine purpose for their writing will encourage them to make more of an effort, give them an opportunity to express their own views and, at times, offer the teacher a window onto their world. Here is an example, from a Geography Unit.

Case Study: 'Connecting ourselves to the world'

Children recorded a weekly news item from both local and international news. Many of the issues raised offered opportunities for pupils to expand their own ideas and offer a genuinely personal response which subsequently generated a high standard of writing. For example, in the same week, two children responded in very different ways, as Figures 7.1 and 7.2 show.

The children's writing is reproduced exactly as they originally wrote it.

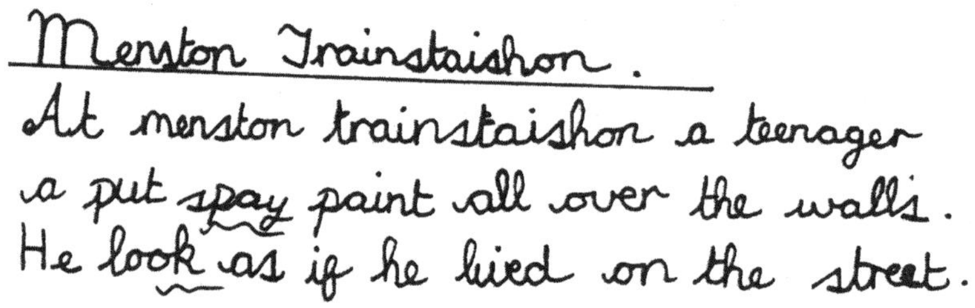

> Menston Trainstaishon.
> At menston trainstaishon a teenager
> a put spay paint all over the walls.
> He look as if he lived on the street.

Figure 7.1 Francesca's News Item, 17 December 2004

> A new road bridge has been built
> in the south of france. It is the
> highest bridge in yurep It cost
> £400,000,000 to bild.
> it was desingned by am man from
> Englend. Fire works went off
> when the bridge was opend

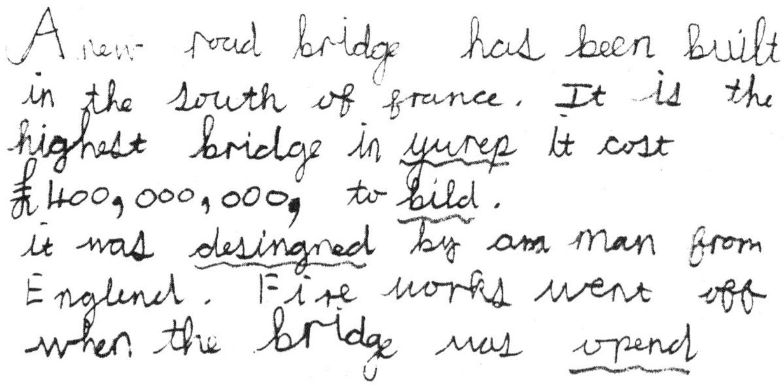

Figure 7.2 Jenny's News Item, 17 December 2004

The activity also allowed children to show their own perspectives on huge international events. Figure 7.3 shows what Jenny wrote about the tsunami which struck the Indian Ocean on Boxing Day, 2004.

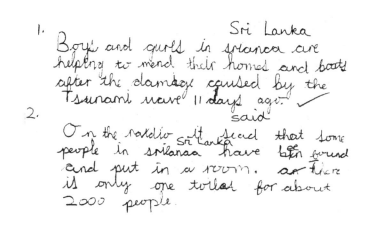

Figure 7.3   Jenny's News Item, 7 January 2005

As we suggested in Chapter 2, stories can provide inspiration for a whole range of writing activities. A bilingual text or story which the minority ethnic pupil can relate to can be used as a stimulus, placing the child in the role of 'expert'. Children can rewrite the story in their own words. The story can be narrated to construct a storyboard with extra dialogue and illustrations. Bilingual texts can also promote language and cultural awareness among 'monolingual' children, and help make links between home and school. Here is what a parent wrote in her child's reading record after sharing a dual language text with him:

> 'We had some fun with this! James read each page in English and I read the same page in Urdu.'

Language and cultural awareness through writing

Writing about festivals

In increasing an awareness of cultural diversity, it is useful to highlight different festivals. This will help communication between different groups in school and community. Having an awareness of each other will combat negative attitudes at school.

Inspire children to write from topics such as the following:

- A family photograph of Eid day
- An artefact from home or school
- Opening a box or school bag
- Historical data
- Information from current affairs.

The more we make the writing topic 'real' for children, the better. I use my personal experiences to help children create a link and share their cultural diversity. For example, I have used my own experiences to help all children understand the month of fasting and Eid ul Fitr. This, in turn, allows Muslim children in the class to feel valued and helps to break down barriers. Before the month of Ramadan, covering work from the PHSCHE and RE units, I share information and facts about myself. I display and discuss the special vocabulary, such as:

Muslims   Eid   Mosque   fasting   praying
helping the poor   breaking the fast   new moon   half moon
Eid Mubarak   decorating hands   henna   Muhammad
celebration   thinking about others   sunrise   sunset

I display pictures of Islamic artefacts, ask children to bring things in from home, such as prayer mats, calendars, Eid cards, food, Islamic patterns on tiles and photographs and pottery with Arabic scriptures.

A variety of writing and creative activities can be incorporated into the planning, for example:

- Stories about the Prophet Muhammad
- Explaining the importance of fasting
- Similarities and differences between different festivals, for example linking Lent and the festival of Christmas
- Festival celebrated by different children, for example a fact sheet about my Muslim friend – Zakariyah.

In one lesson, after discussion, the children wrote facts about me as their teacher. From these next examples, we can see the kinds of links that they made.

Case Study: Linking Eid and Christmas

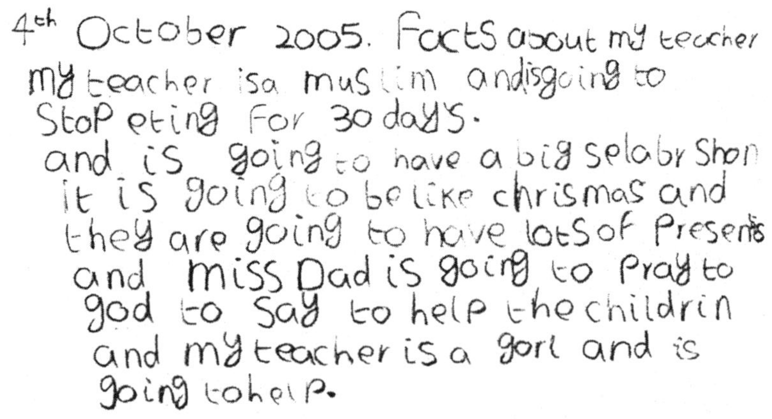

4th October 2005. Facts about my teacher
my teacher isa muslim andisgoing to
StoP eting For 30 day's.
and is going to have a big selabr shon
it is going to be like chrismas and
they are going to have lots of Presents
and miss Dad is going to Pray to
god to Say to help the childrin
and my teacher is a gorl and is
going tohelP.

Figure 7.4   Harrison's writing about his teacher

After considerable discussion at school about Eid, Harrison, a 6-year-old child, went home and discussed the festival with his family.

Another child, Bradley returned to school with an Eid card for me, which showed how his family had also become involved in the discussion and making of the card. Part of it was done by his mother and part by himself.

TO miss Dadd

HaPPY
Eid

#

Inshallah may Allah
accept your fast
and always be with you.
Love from

Bradley and family
X X

Eid Mubarak

Figure 7.5   An Eid card made by Bradley and his family

In writing, pupils like to use the correct technical and specialist vocabulary of different subjects. The next example was done by 6-year-olds without any adult help. The new vocabulary the children used for themselves (which had previously been introduced in discussion) was: *Eid Mubarak* and *henna*.

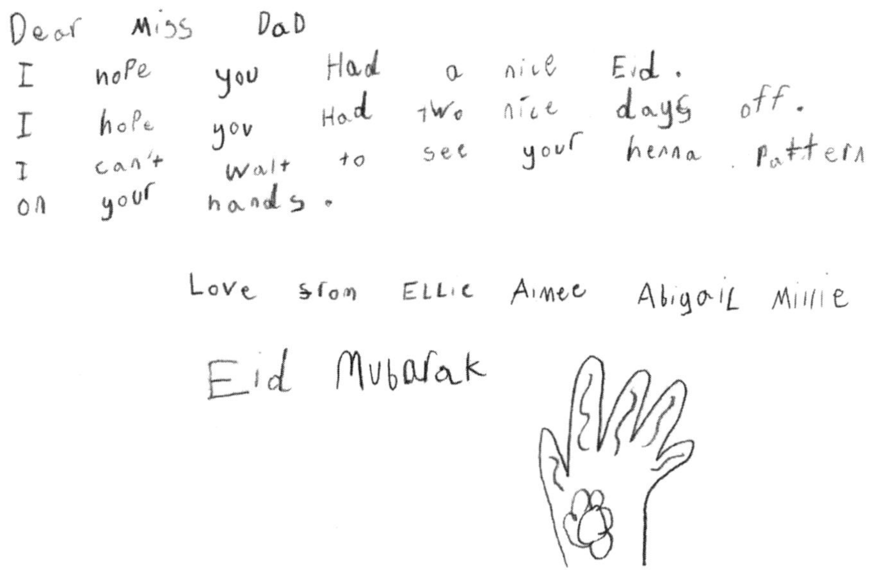

Figure 7.6   Aimee, Millie, Ellie and Abigail's card

Words of the week

To promote language awareness, helping both 'monolingual' and bilingual pupils to see similarities between different languages and English, I introduce words from different cultures as a 'words of the week' challenge. Children are given a set of three words each week, which they record in their diaries. Throughout the week the children are encouraged to use a dictionary to find the meanings of the words, and to use them in conversations with adults or in their written work. Examples of words of the week are:

God   Deity   Supreme   Being
Carnival   Mela   Fete
Divali   Ramadan   Hanuka

'Bilingual' writing

If children have some knowledge of literacy in their first language, this can be used as a tool to help them develop literacy in English. If they already have a well-established language system, they can apply the skills of their first language when they are learning English as their second language. Sometimes, children make links for themselves, such as Haleema, whose drawing of a plane in Figure 7.7 shows her knowledge of two ways of writing 'PIA'.

Constructing bilingual texts can help children recognize similarities in sound patterns when we are introducing the alphabet and letter sounds in English.

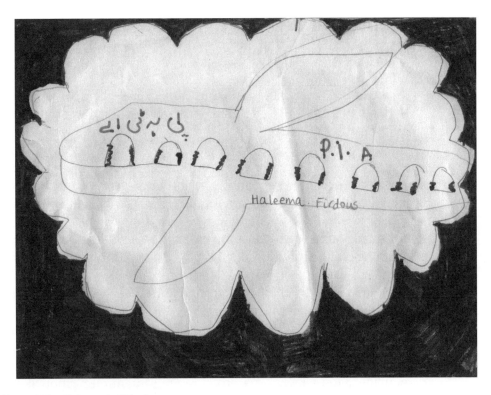

Figure 7.7   Haleema's PIA plane

Figure 7.8 shows a worksheet with Urdu letters and sounds. In recognizing the Urdu letters and sounds the bilingual pupil can use the ideas to match these to letter sounds and objects in English.

Figure 7.8   Worksheet for matching Urdu letters and sounds with English sounds

PROMOTING DIVERSITY AND COHESION THROUGH LINKING SCHOOLS

Since 2001, the Schools Linking Project has been working in many primary schools in Bradford. The aims are to establish positive and sustainable relationships between pupils who attend schools in different parts of the district, so that pupils from diverse backgrounds have opportunities to meet and explore their commonalities and differences. It is hoped that, by addressing issues of social diversity and cohesion in this way, we will be equipping young people to become skilled 'intercultural navigators' and ambassadors for a more peaceful, productive and cohesive community.

An important factor that the linking project addresses is where there may be just one child of a different ethnic background to that of his or her classmates. If such a class meets with a class from a school where the majority of the children are from different backgrounds, this can be a very positive factor in the 'isolated' child's learning experience.

Linking schools has advantages for all children through enabling them to meet and mix in 'normal' circumstances, doing what they would do every day. Spending a school day together incorporates a range of formal and informal activities, and allows for a broad range of communication skills to be encouraged and developed. This is an important aspect of the work and has a positive impact on achievement as well as social cohesion. Careful planning and preparation based upon a clear understanding of the teaching and learning of communication skills is crucial.

Through linking, pupils of all ethnic backgrounds have the opportunity to explore the curriculum from different cultural perspectives. For example, studying the Second World War in the Schools Linking Project has become an exciting opportunity to interview older people, not only from a pupil's own community, but also from other communities in the city. This opens up exciting and meaningful possibilities for genuine enquiry and builds pupils' confidence in purposeful language use. It is particularly interesting to see pupils whose first and only language is English grow in admiration and respect for their peers who are able to translate the older people's stories, which are often told in other languages.

An additional advantage of links between schools with ethnically, culturally and linguistically diverse populations is that staff can develop new skills by working alongside one another and with different pupils. This was something we noticed very early on in the project. It is not always a comfortable experience, but – like all real learning – it is extremely worthwhile.

This work, by its nature, throws the school ethos into sharp relief. Where a school is welcoming and has a strong and positive relationship with the community it serves, everyone has a stake and an interest in the linking work and it comes more easily to all involved. Classes hold assemblies to share the work they have done with their link school, parents get involved and children feel positive and secure about making new relationships. Through involvement in the project, some schools become aware that there is work to do in developing their own ethos, and support is available for this to happen.

How the project works

There are five key factors in the organization and development of the Schools Linking Project:

- Central coordination
- Partnership working between teachers and creative sector workers
- Training and support for teachers and schools
- Financial support
- Internal and external evaluation.

Central coordination is important, particularly in a district as large and diverse as Bradford. It allows for key messages to be disseminated and shared, for a pool of supportive creative workers to be linked to schools and for training and support materials to be developed. Crucially, it also provides a steer and a listening ear when schools need support.

We discovered that the most powerful tool for learning and teaching across the curriculum in a culturally diverse and challenging way was to use creativity. For example:

- Drama can facilitate work on immigration
- Art can provide a way of expressing relationships and understanding experiences
- Dance and other physical activity can develop new skills and teamwork.

We discovered also that this does not come naturally in all classrooms – good partnership working requires thought, planning and training. Central to all of this is the emphasis on communication, at three levels:

- Between the children
- Between the adults
- Between the adults and the children.

The creative activities facilitate this communication, first by providing a stimulus that is not necessarily language-based but requires a linguistic response and secondly because it helps everyone to find ways of expressing and developing affective and not only cognitive responses.

Training days have been developed incorporating themes such as the use of cultural venues and working collaboratively with a range of different practitioners, as well as addressing organizational and practical issues and issues of race and cultural awareness. Feedback from teachers has led us to see that this support is essential. Training days also provide important opportunities for the teachers to network and learn from each other. Further training is also offered to whole schools on any issues that have been raised for them by participating in the project.

The following two brief case studies provide a snapshot of the project in operation.

Case Study: The Schools Linking Project in Primary Schools G and E

These two schools were pioneers of the Schools Linking Project in 2001–2, carrying out drama and art activities at Cartwright Hall, one of Bradford's main cultural venues. The project has grown from the model developed organically with them.

School G is an inner city primary, with approximately 98% pupils of Pakistani heritage. Many start school with English as an additional language. The school is a beacon school for inclusion, a resourced school for hearing-impaired pupils and has an impressive achievement record, particularly in KS 1. It was in the pursuit of continuing this through KS 2 that, in 2001, when the project started, innovative language work was being explored.

School E is a suburban school, with the majority of its pupils of white British backgrounds. Also a beacon school and with consistently high achievement, one of its major strengths is in the use of drama across the curriculum, particularly to promote high attainment through writing.

These two schools came together to explore what they had to offer each other, in terms of learning and teaching communication skills and of building positive and sustainable relationships between their communities at a time when this seemed both difficult and crucial for the wider Bradford community.

All the adults involved were apprehensive and yet hopeful about this work. But no one was prepared for how eagerly the children grasped the opportunity and how clearly they expressed their views. No-one told the children directly about the aims of the project. But after a few meetings, they knew. They told us that everyone should be doing this, so that 'we won't have riots any more in our city'. The 10-year-old boy who said this was the only minority ethnic child in the class at School E. The project enabled him to speak out and show us as adults that we have to have the courage of our convictions. The teachers realized that working with the link school had given him the opportunity to explore and articulate his feelings of isolation in a constructive way.

The following year, the two schools spent their first day together at an outdoor activity centre to develop trust and confidence. The teachers followed this up by reflecting with the children what it was that made that day so successful in terms of relationship building and task completion. The children were able to explore the themes of collaboration and cooperation and then test their hypotheses by inventing, designing, making and playing board games in pairs the next time they met their link class.

These two schools have gone from strength to strength in their relationship. Each year, one year group is chosen to be involved and all 60 pupils in the year group are included, even if they have additional educational, physical or emotional needs. In fact, the emphasis on inclusion has been a strength in this link; some children at School E have been inspired to learn sign language to make sure that they can communicate with the hearing-impaired children at School

G. One boy at School E, who is autistic and found the linking experience difficult at first, excelled in learning sign language and looked forward to subsequent meetings with great enthusiasm.

Case Study: The Schools Linking Project in Primary Schools B and S

These two schools have linked for two years and are also very committed to linking as one of a range of strategies in both schools to combat racism and to raise awareness of cultural diversity.

School B is in an area of the city that is unusual in its diversity, so the school itself works hard to draw on its own cultural mix in a positive way. School S is in a semi-rural setting, with an all-white population, and is very keen to broaden the social experience of its pupils. Together they are developing a piece of work in RE called *Doorways*, which explores entrances to different places of worship and also leads to imaginative work, encouraging the children to articulate the way they inhabit different worlds at school, home, place of worship, sometimes other houses and even in other countries. These children have developed an extremely mature approach to issues of identity, community and racism. They can explain how they will describe themselves differently depending on the context they are in. One child wrote: *It's good to mix because when we grow up we'll be with different people all at the same time, we won't be with our religion people.*

They work with their school councils to combat racism and other bullying in their schools, bringing the Citizenship curriculum to life in their everyday practices.

Some factors common to all schools successfully involved in the linking project have been identified:

- A clear understanding from the leadership that the aims of linking are fundamental to the education of their pupils
- An awareness of the importance of linking to the extended community of the school.
- Good planning, rooted in the normal curriculum and enhanced by creative aspects as appropriate.
- A belief among teachers that this is a valuable and crucial aspect of their work.

Teachers all give willingly of their time and energy and are rewarded by the heartwarming moments they witness when children who would not normally meet are sitting chatting side by side while completing a task. Through their involvement, many teachers have found a renewed sense of purpose. The children often comment how happy they are to make new friends and to discover that children who they expected to be so different are not very different after all.

More details of the Schools Linking Project are available from the website, listed at the end of the chapter.

CONCLUSION

The main points covered in this chapter are summarized in the box, which provides a set of key principles for promoting a positive ethos and supporting bilingual learners in 'mainly white' schools.

Summary: Principles for promoting a positive ethos in schools

1. To succeed in school, all pupils need to feel that they belong, and that they are recognized and valued for who they are.
2. In 'mainly white' schools, bilingual pupils may feel isolated. Small actions and attention to detail can help them feel secure and that they belong.
3. Teachers can use their own personal experiences and knowledge in powerful ways to relate to their pupils and help them feel they belong in school.
4. Writing is a powerful tool to promote a positive ethos in school and to highlight pupils' own attitudes and responses to different issues.
5. There is great value in primary schools linking with each other to build positive relationships and provide pupils with first-hand experiences of diversity.

 Useful websites

www.schoolslinkingproject.org
www.standards.dfes.gov.uk/ethnicminorities/raising_achievement/
www.naldic.org.uk/

Glossary

accent	ways of speaking that are special to a person or group, region or nation
additive bilingualism	new languages are learnt in addition to the languages already spoken and written
BICS	*basic interpersonal communication skills*: according to Cummins (and others), these are skills in conversing and communicating which language learners develop fairly quickly and easily
CALP	*cognitive academic language proficiency*: these are the deeper, more complex uses of language which take longer to develop and are essential for academic success
contexts	the 'surroundings' to the learning activity, including the physical setting, the language(s) being used and the relationships between the participants in the activity
codeswitching	a normal aspect of bilingualism; the facility to move naturally from one language to another in conversation
dialect	a variety of language which is special to a particular region or group of people, differing from the standard in vocabulary and/or grammar
EAL	*English as an additional language*: the current 'official' terminology for bilingual pupils
ethnicity	the distinctive attributes, such as language, cultural practices and so on, that identify people as belonging to particular social and cultural groups
identity	the attributes that make up each person's individuality and sense of self
metalinguistic awareness	the perception of language as a code, made up of various elements and the capacity to talk about it in this way
repertoires	the collection of skills and knowledge in language(s) that each individual possesses

scaffolding	the support provided by the context to facilitate learning
standard English	the form of English generally connected with educational and social success
transitional bilingualism	as new languages are learnt, the languages already spoken and written are not used and are gradually forgotten

Bibliography

Bastiani, John and Wolfendale, Sheila (eds) (1996) *Home – School Work in Britain: Review, Reflection and Development*. London: David Fulton.

Bolton, Gavin (1995) (with Dorothy Heathcote) *Drama for Learning: Dorothy Heathcote's Mantle of the Expert Approach to Education*. Portsmouth, NJ: Heinemann.

Brock, Avril (ed.) (1996) *Into the Enchanted Forest – Language, Drama and Science in Primary Schools*. Stoke-on-Trent: Trentham Books.

Conteh, Jean (2003) *Succeeding in Diversity: Culture, Language and Learning in Primary Classrooms*. Stoke-on-Trent: Trentham Books.

Cummins, Jim (2001) *Negotiating Identities: Education for Empowerment in a Diverse Society*, 2nd edn. Ontario, CA: California Association for Bilingual Education.

Dulay, Heidi, Burt, Marina and Krashen, Stephen (1982) *Language Two*. Oxford: Oxford University Press.

Fellowes, Alex (2001) *Bilingual Shakespeare: A Practical Approach for Teachers*. Stoke-on-Trent: Trentham Books.

Gibbons, Pauline (1991) *Learning to Learn in a Second Language. NSW, Australia*: PETA.

Gibbons, Pauline (2002) *Scaffolding Language, Scaffolding Learning: Teaching Second Language Learners in the Mainstream Classroom*. London: Heinemann.

Gregory, Eve, Long, Susie and Volk, Dinah (eds) (2004) *Many Pathways to Literacy: Young Children Learning with Siblings, Grandparents, Peers and Communities*. London: RoutledgeFarmer.

Grugeon, Elizabeth, Hubbard, Lorraine, Smith, Carol and Dawes, Lyn (2001) *Teaching Speaking and Listening in the Primary School*. London: David Fulton.

Hall, Deryn, Griffiths, Dominic, Haslam, Liz and Wilkin, Yvonne (2001) *Assessing the Needs of Bilingual Pupils: Living in Two Languages*, 2nd edn. London: David Fulton.

Hodson, Pam and Jones, Deborah (2001) *Teaching Children to Write: The Process Approach*. London: David Fulton.

McWilliam, Norah (1998) *What's in a Word?* Stoke-on-Trent: Trentham Books.

Moll, Luis et al. (1992) Funds of Knowledge for Teaching: Using a Qualitative Approach to Connect Homes and Classrooms, *Theory into Practice*, 31 (2), pp. 132–141.

NALDIC (National Association for Language Development in the Curriculum) (1999) *The Distinctiveness of English as an Additional Language: A Cross-curriculum Discipline*. Working Paper 5.

Neelands, Jonathan (1984) *Making Sense of Drama: A Guide to Classroom Practice*. Oxford: Heinemann Educational Books.

QCA (2000) *Curriculum Guidance for the Foundation Stage*. London: DfEE.

Wells, G. and Chang-Wells, G.L. (1992) *Constructing Knowledge Together: Classrooms as Centres of Inquiry and Literacy*. Portsmouth, NH: Heinemann.

Wrigley, T. (2003) *Schools of Hope: A New Agenda for School Improvement*. Stoke-on-Trent: Trentham Books.

Useful Websites

www.multiverse.ac.uk/
www.naldic.org.uk/
www.qca.org.uk
www.schoolslinkingproject.org
www.standardsdfes.gov.uk/ethnicminorities/raising_achievement/

Index